The Lionel Messi Story

Luciano Wernicke

THE LIONEL MESSI STORY

How One Man Revolutionized Major League Soccer

Meyer & Meyer Sport

British Library Cataloguing in Publication Data
A catalogue record for this book is available from the British Library

The Lionel Messi Story
Maidenhead: Meyer & Meyer Sport (UK) Ltd., 2026
ISBN 978-1-78255-290-1

Aachen, Auckland, Beirut, Cairo, Cape Town, Dubai, Hägendorf, Hong Kong, Indianapolis, Maidenhead, Manila, New Delhi, Singapore, Sydney, Tehran, Vienna

Member of the World Sport Publishers' Association (WSPA), www.w-s-p-a.org

Printed by Versa Press, East Peoria, IL
www.versapress.com
Printed in the United States of America
ISBN 978-1-78255-290-1
Email: info@m-m-sports.com
www.thesportspublisher.com

Credits
Cover and interior design: Anja Elsen
Layout: Anja Elsen
Cover image: picture alliance / Hans Lucas / David Himbert
Managing editor: Elizabeth Evans
Copy editor: Sarah Tomblin, www.sarahtomblinediting.com

Manufacturer under the GPSR
Meyer & Meyer Fachverlag und Buchhandel GmbH
Von-Coels-Str. 390
52080 Aachen, Germany
www.dersportverlag.de

PREFACE

TIME magazine's "Athlete of the Year 2023" was surprisingly not a football, baseball, or basketball player (the three most popular sports in the United States), but rather a soccer player. Soccer, although growing in popularity, does not register with most US sports fans. *TIME*'s chosen athlete was the Argentine Lionel Messi, who though he was the winner of the 2022 Qatar World Cup with the Albiceleste national team, only participated in a quarter of the official matches of the Major League Soccer (MLS) season, the professional league in the US and Canada. In addition, his team—the Miami International Soccer Club (Inter Miami, on the sport's map)—did not qualify for the playoffs of the main American competition, and only won one title in that first half year with Leo: the Leagues Cup, a minor competition compared with the MLS or the Concacaf Champions Cup, the top club-level tournament of the Confederation of North, Central America and the Caribbean Football Association.

Why did *TIME* choose Messi over heroes like Kansas City Chiefs quarterback Patrick Mahomes, Denver Nuggets' Serbian center Nikola Jokić, or Texas Rangers shortstop Corey Seager? Was it for helping the Florida franchise gain its first medal? Or because of his "undiminished talent" as the magazine itself described him? No. He *TIME* chose him because Leo "set a new standard for athlete leverage and empowerment." "At 36, two decades into his unparalleled career, Messi provided a singular stimulus to soccer in America. Attendance, ticket prices, merchandise sales, and viewership soared. His games took on the feel of a religious revival," the publication explained in its article. *TIME* said that the United States, a country where sports often offer huge profits to franchises and their sponsors but which had not yet absorbed the passion for soccer, hosted three major international tournaments in the next three years: Copa America in 2024, the FIFA Club World Cup in 2025, and the grandest of them all, the World Cup, in 2026, Hosting these tournaments would likely attract more fans, but as *TIME* noted, "Messi is an accelerant."

"With the most revered and influential athlete on the planet playing in Miami for at least the next two years, still performing at the top of his game—he won another Ballon d'Or as the world's player of the year, his eighth, in late October—the U.S. is now a soccer nation. A fútbol nation," *TIME* said.

Indeed, Messi's arrival at Inter Miami in June 2023 shook everything up. Many previously lackluster stadiums placed the "sold out" sign in their windows. Soldier Field, home of Chicago Fire FC, which has an average of 15,000 spectators per game, hosted 62,000 fans for the South Florida team in October 2023; in April 2024, Sporting Kansas City, which plays its home games at 18,500-seat Children's Mercy Park, moved its game against Inter to the Kansas City Chiefs' Arrowhead Stadium—all 76,500 seats were sold out.

The ratings showed a sudden and steep increase, and the pink jerseys with number 10 on the back flew off the shelves. According to *The New York Times*, sales of Lionel Messi's jersey "have surpassed every benchmark adidas could have imagined," exceeding the company's production capacity. But the frenzy was not only in North American territory; the shirts (original and the others . . .) flooded the streets and fields around the world. Newspaper reports highlighted that pink shirts—and the black ones with pink trims—had even found their way *en masse* into English playing fields—until then, an area exclusive to deep-rooted, traditional local clubs, such as Manchester United, Liverpool, or Chelsea. Hurricane Messi had not just swept away the North American crowds.

The MLS, previously an uninspiring league for South American, European, and Asian palates, became a global phenomenon, thanks to its new star. According to *TIME*, on the day of Messi's debut at Inter Miami, Apple—the owner of MLS television rights—added around 110,000 American subscriptions to its MLS Season Pass service, but the numbers in Argentina, Brazil, Mexico, and Europe "went from basically zero to moving the needle in a huge way," according to Eddy Cue, Senior Vice President of Services for Apple.

Who is Lionel Messi? For many people, he is simply the best soccer player of all time. For others, at least one of the three greatest legends of this sport, along with the Brazilian Pelé—three-time world champion in 1958, 1962, and 1970—and another Argentine, Diego Maradona, who shone in the 1980s and 1990s. For everyone, the most extraordinary star of the twenty-first century. His sporting achievements include 46 titles (including a World Cup and four European Champions Leagues) and eight Ballon d'Ors, the highest individual honor in soccer.

To help you fully know and understand this sporting legend, this book provides a vivid and illuminating insight into his history: his beginnings, his exploits, his anecdotes, his thoughts, and other soccer celebrities' thoughts about him. Definitely, everything that can be told and explained about Lionel Messi. Because, to know the rest, there are no words—you just have to watch him play.

PROFESSIONAL SUMMARY

Lionel Messi is one of the most important players in the entire history of soccer. Left-handed, skilled, and versatile—he can play as a midfielder or as a forward—he has won dozens of titles with FC Barcelona (Spain), Paris Saint-Germain (PSG) (France), and Inter Miami CF (US), and the World Cup with the Argentina national team. He received eight Ballon d'Ors, the highest individual distinction for soccer athletes. Messi is known as *La Pulga* (The Flea, nickname that emerged during his childhood because he was very short as a result of a hormonal deficiency), *El Mesías* (The Messiah), or simply *Leo*, a nickname he received during his youth stage in the Catalan team.

BIRTHDAY

June 24, 1987: Lionel Andrés Messi was born at 4:20 p.m. in the Garibaldi Italian Hospital of Rosario, Argentine province of Santa Fe. He weighed 3 kilograms and 600 grams, and measured 47 centimeters.

FAMILY

Leo is the third of four siblings: Rodrigo and Matías are the oldest, María Sol is the youngest. His parents are Jorge Messi and Celia Cuccittini. The Flea began playing soccer in a small club in Rosario called Agrupación Infantil Abanderado Grandoli, located in the Saladillo neighborhood. One afternoon in 1991, Lionel and his maternal grandmother, Celia Ramona Olivera, accompanied Rodrigo and Matías to the club. The Messis settled in to one of the stands to watch their respective matches and noticed that the 1986 class team was a player down because one of the kids had not shown up. Celia approached the coach, Salvador Aparicio, and suggested that Lionel, who was only four years old and younger than the other boys in that group, could complete the team. Aparicio refused:

"He is very small," the coach said. "Put him on the team, he will save you," his grandmother insisted. After a few minutes of arguments, the coach agreed. That day, Grandoli's 1986 team won thanks to two great goals from its new star: Leo Messi.

My grandmother Celia satisfied our every whim. Me, my brothers and cousins fought over sleeping at her house, she pampered us all. I dedicate my goals and my triumphs to her, but she left before seeing me succeed. That's what annoys me the most. She saw me so many times as a child and never saw me succeed."
(Lionel Messi's grief was evident in an interview given to the newspaper *Mundo Deportivo*.)

EDUCATION

Lionel Messi completed his primary studies at the General Las Heras school. "He was shy and quiet," said his fifth-grade teacher, Andrea Sosa. He was not exceptional as a student—in tests, he used to receive help from a former classmate, Cintia Arellano, who gave him the correct answers—but he was notable for his soccer ability. Although he went to the institute in the afternoon, a group of students from his morning classes invited him to join the team to compete in an interschool tournament. Messi accepted and the squad became champions without losing a game.

JUEGUITOS

A Rosario legend claims that when Messi was a child, one summer afternoon someone challenged him: "If you do a hundred keepie-uppies [juggling by hitting the ball with feet, legs, shoulders or head without letting it touch the ground, a skill also known as *freestyle*], I'll give you an ice cream." The Flea made it to 1,100 without losing control of the ball, so he received 11 ice creams—one for himself and the others for 10 of his friends.

NEWELL'S OLD BOYS

On March 21, 1994, after excelling at Abanderado Grandoli, Lionel Messi agreed to be signed by the club of which he was a fan: Newell's Old Boys. The Flea competed for six years for the red and black club in the children's categories in tournaments organized by the Asociación Rosarina de Fútbol (Rosario Football Association) for teams made up of seven players. During that period, Messi achieved some remarkable statistics: 234 goals in 176 games. Thanks to that barrage of goals, Newell's won all the championships, and the team, led by The Messiah, received the nickname *The 87 Machine*. Leo's first "international" title was the Friendship Cup, a quadrangular tournament organized in early 1996 by the Cantolao Sports Academy of Peru. Newell's destroyed its two rivals 10-0 and 7-1, with an outstanding performance by their number 10, who was only eight years old and recovering from food poisoning. Despite being sick, Messi scored seven goals in the first game and three in the second.

NUMBERS

Lionel Messi's goals in the Newell's youth divisions.

Year	Games	Goals	Average
1994	29	40	1.38
1995	30	36	1.2
1996	27	36	1.33
1997	36	40	1.11
1998	25	27	1.08
1999	29	55	1.9
Total	**176**	**234**	**1.33**

BICYCLE

In an interview, Celia Cuccittini, the star's mother, revealed that before a final of a tournament offering new bicycles as a prize for all the members of the champion team, Lionel—who was six years old and already playing for Newell's—was stuck in the bathroom at home because the door latch was stuck. Leo shouted for his parents or his brothers to rescue him, but everyone had come out to watch the match, convinced that the young prodigal player was already on the field. Desperate, the little boy broke the glass of the bathroom window and escaped from his prison. When he arrived on the soccer court, his team was losing 0-2. Messi entered the game in the second half and, in just 20 minutes, scored three goals. Newell's won 3-2 and the hero returned home, pedaling his new bicycle.

MEMORABLE DATE

Boys club. The red and black team beat Pablo VI 6-0, and their new idol scored four goals.

GROWTH HORMONES

In early 1997, one of the members of Newell's Medical Department asked endocrinologist Diego Schwarzstein, who also worked with the club, to examine Lionel Messi, whose physical development had slowed down. "We are going to send you a boy who is the best we have in the children divisions, but he is very small. We need you to help him grow!" the Newell's doctor begged Schwarzstein. The specialist discovered a glandular deficit preventing normal development of the body of the little soccer player, who was about to turn 10 years old, and recommended a treatment with growth hormones to inject periodically using a syringe known as a "pen." From his 125 centimeters of height, Lionel expressed only one concern: "Doctor, will I be able to play soccer?" "You're going to be taller than Maradona," Schwarzstein guaranteed him. He was not wrong: thanks to the treatment, Leo reached 1.69 meters and surpassed Diego by four centimeters.

For my old man I never play well. When I was little I scored four goals and I didn't play well: he always had something to say to me or criticize me. That made me want to improve myself more, so that the next game would come and he wouldn't say anything to me."

(Lionel Messi, interviewed by the TyC Sports channel in 2013)

PASIÓN ROJINEGRA

The supplement *Pasión Rojinegra* (red and black passion) of the Rosario newspaper *La Capital* was the first media to publish a journalistic interview with Lionel Messi. Reporter Érica Pizzuto, responsible for news about the children's divisions of Newell's, produced the report. Pizzuto had designed a questionnaire for the boys in the 1986 category, with which Leo had begun training, which she then published weekly in a section called "Today we present." The interview with Messi appeared on September 3, 2000. The most interesting questions and answers are:

A hobby: Listening to music.

A type of music: *Cuarteto (genre of popular music native to the Argentine city of Córdoba) and cumbia.*

A book: *The Bible.*

A movie: *Baby's Day Out.*

Another sport: *Handball.*

One meal: *Chicken with sauce.*

Career goal: *Physical education teacher.*

One objective: *Finish high school.*

A sadness: *The death of my grandmother.*

An ambition: *To play in Newell's first team.*

A memory: *When my grandmother took me to play soccer for the first time.*

A dream: *Play for the national team.*

FLORIDA

In 1998, a tourism company organized a trip to Florida for a group of kids from Newell's minor divisions to visit the Disney parks and play friendly games at a Palm Beach soccer academy. The owner of the company asked his secretary to call Jorge Messi because his son, chosen as the best by his colleagues, would travel for free. But the woman got confused and she called Jorge *Melzi*, father of a boy named Julián who was also a member of the Rosario club's children's division. Because of that mistake, Leo missed his first trip to Florida; Julián took his place.

MEDICATION

Excited by the promise of growth, Lionel quickly learned how to inject himself with hormones, prepare the doses, and preserve the medication that would help his body develop. "At first, they hurt, but then I familiarized with them," he stated in an interview. The medicine had to be kept refrigerated, and he had to place it in a special container, with ice, when he slept at a friend's house or had to travel to compete. During the year 2000, the economic crisis that affected Argentina directly impacted Messi's progress: the government postponed the reimbursement payment for medical procedures and pharmaceutical supplies to the unions' medical services. The association linked to Jorge Messi's work stopped providing coverage for the medication, which was equivalent to US$1,000 a month. Jorge asked Newell's to help him pay for his son's treatment, but the club's leaders refused. Desperate, Leo and his father accepted a trial at River Plate, a powerful institution that could afford the cost of the medication. However, the problem was not resolved because Newell's did not want to approve the player's transfer. A beacon of hope appeared on the other side of the Atlantic Ocean. The brightness shone from the Camp Nou stadium in the city of Barcelona.

LA MASÍA

Thanks to FIFA regulations that enabled the free international transfer of underage amateur players, Jorge Messi secured a trial at La Masía, the FC Barcelona training academy, through an agent. Jorge and Lionel traveled to Catalonia on September 17, 2000. In his first trial, *La Pulga* amazed the technical secretary of the *culé* team, Carles Rexach, with his quality and dribbling skills, despite his small height and the challenge of completing his trial in front of boys two to three years older than the young man from Rosario. Fascinated, Rexach recommended that the club immediately sign the rough diamond from Argentina. In the first official agreement, FC Barcelona agreed to pay for its new star's hormonal treatment, plus a "scholarship" or grant of about €5,000 per month, in addition to accommodation costs for an apartment. Jorge Messi was also hired as a "match reporter"—a "job" that justified the family's residence in Spain and the international transfer of the young player. Although Newell's Old Boys at first refused to release Leo's transfer, the club finally had to agree due FIFA's intervention. Thus, the Rosario star was cleared to play for the Catalan team.

MEMORABLE DATE

September 23, 2000: Lionel Messi attended FC Barcelona's Camp Nou for the first time, invited by the directors of the Catalan institution. That day, the *Blaugrana* team beat Racing de Santander 3-1 with three Dutch goals: two scored by Patrick Kluivert and one by Marc Overmars.

CONTRACT

The first association between Lionel Messi and FC Barcelona was a handwritten contract drafted by Carles Rexach on a paper napkin in the cafeteria of the Royal Pompeia Tennis Society, where the director and the adviser of the Catalan club, José María Minguella, had a meeting with Leo's father, Jorge. That unusual document, which would later be replaced by a formal contract, remained in the possession of the sports agent: it is presumed that he keeps it stored in a safe deposit box at the Crèdit Andorrà bank. Minguella, meanwhile, is known for having advised FC Barcelona to include two of the three best soccer players in history—both Argentinians—into the first team; in addition to recommending signing Messi in 1982, he managed the hiring of Diego Maradona.

No matter what happens along the way, you always have to try." (Lionel Messi, in statements to *Televisión Pública* of Argentina, in June 2023)

In an interview in 2005 for *TyC Sports*, Lionel Messi complained about the cold reception he experienced in his early training sessions at La Masía. His first teammates ignored him, speaking among themselves in Catalan so that he would not understand what they were talking about. In games, they didn't pass him the ball and insulted him if he made a mistake. Some, behind his back, referred to him with a derogatory nickname: dwarf. Through goals and dribbles, the little Argentine player changed animosity for admiration. "Then they opened to me and the situation changed," *La Pulga* said. He also revealed that months after his arrival, one of the boys with whom he became friends confided in him that a coach from the youth divisions had told his pupils, without Leo hearing: "This one who comes from outside cannot stay, you must kick him." That same coach was, however, won over by the kid who turned him, unintentionally, into a winning coach.

TRIVIA

Upon arriving in Barcelona, Lionel Messi carried with him a VHS video cassette with a recording in which he played 113 *jueguitos* in a row with an orange, 140 with a tennis ball, and 29 with a ping-pong ball.

NEW BEGINNING

The Messi family settled in an apartment in the Les Corts neighborhood, on Gran Vía de Carlos III, just a 15-minute walk from La Masía. The move was not easy: Leo's brothers couldn't settle in the new city and returned to Rosario with their mother. Only Lionel and his father remained in Barcelona. In a television interview in 2018, *La Pulga* revealed: "My dad asked me: 'What do we do? You have the decision.' I told him: 'I want to stay,' convinced despite how difficult it was. But I saw that the possibility [of reaching the *Barça* first team] was real." However, he acknowledged that that period was not easy: "I locked myself in the room and cried. I didn't want my dad to see me. I missed a lot."

NUMBERS

Players who have appeared in the most FIFA World Cups games:

Player (Country)	Matches	World Cups
1 Lionel Messi (Argentina)	26	2006, 2010, 2014, 2018, 2022
2 Lothar Matthäus (Germany)	25	1982, 1986, 1990, 1994, 1998
3 Miroslav Klose (Germany)	24	2002, 2006, 2010, 2014
4 Paolo Maldini (Italy)	23	1990, 1994, 1998, 2002
5 Cristiano Ronaldo (Portugal)	22	2006, 2010, 2014, 2018, 2022

SCHOOL DAYS

Lionel Messi continued his secondary studies, from the second to fourth year, at the Lleó (León) XIII school in Sant Gervasi, in the northern part of Barcelona. Every morning, Leo arrived at La Masía at 8:30 and boarded a school bus with kids from other Spanish cities who lived in the apartments specially built for the boys who had come from other cities or countries. Upon returning, he would have lunch with them—generally, hamburgers and fries, or, rarely, fish and vegetables—which had helped him endure the departure of his mother and to strengthen friendship bonds. "We sat at the end of the classroom and if we didn't like the class, we would start listening to music. He would listen to cumbia all day," recalled one of his classmates, Víctor Vázquez, who although he did not play in Barça's First Division, had an extensive career, including two MLS clubs: Los Angeles Galaxy and FC Toronto.

Maribel Pascual, who was *La Pulga's* teacher, acknowledged in an interview with the newspaper *Mundo Deportivo* that "study was not his great motivation. He was not bad at drawing or life skills, but it was already clear that his life was soccer. Leo was very humble, not at all arrogant," although sometimes "he let himself be carried away by the group and then he would do more tricks." In statements to *El Gráfico* magazine, Lionel recalled that "in class there were 20 of us from Barça and the last thing we did was study. We drove the teachers crazy." "I was a disaster. I was very lazy, I didn't like it. In reality, I don't know if it was difficult for me or I was lazy, but I was doing poorly in all the subjects," he confessed.

MEMORABLE DATE

March 7, 2001: Lionel Messi played his first official match for FC Barcelona in the boys Infantil B team A. With the number 9 on his shirt, Leo is part of the away team that defeated the Amposta club 0-3.

TWO GAMES AND A GOAL

A week after Lionel Messi's debut on European soil, FC Barcelona hosted Ebre Escola Esportiva at La Masía. With just two minutes of play, the away player Marc Baiges tried to throw a shot, but his left foot missed the ball and hit Leo's left ankle, as he burst in to steal the ball. A snap was heard, and the two teenagers were sprawled on the grass. Baiges sat up, but *La Pulga* did not manage to get up: the unintentional blow had broken his fibula. In his second "official" match with the blue and red shirt, Messi suffered an injury that kept him off the field for three months. But in June, having recovered from the fracture, he injured his left ankle while going down a staircase, spraining a ligament. Thus, his first season at the Barça club was completed with just two games and a single goal.

I have been a Barça fan since Ronaldo played."

(In October 2003, Lionel Messi revealed to the newspaper *Mundo Deportivo* his admiration for the Brazilian striker Ronaldo Luís Nazário de Lima, who wore the red and blue shirt in the 1996/97 season and was champion in two World Cups: US 1994 and Korea-Japan 2002.)

DAD TO THE RESCUE

In the 2002/03 season, Lionel Messi was part of a fabulous team along with several teenagers who would later become stars, such as Cesc Fábregas and Gerard Piqué. FC Barcelona's Cadete B team won La Liga, the Catalunya Cup, and the Spanish Championship undefeated. In a match against Real Club Deportivo Espanyol, Leo received an elbow in the face, which caused a crack in his cheekbone. The doctor recommended that he rest for a few weeks to prevent the injury from being aggravated by another blow and needing surgery. However, Messi begged him to be allowed to play in the final of the Catalan Cup, again against Espanyol, and promised that he would wear a protective mask. The doctor agreed. But, at the beginning of the match, Lionel noticed that it was impossible to play with it attached to his face: "As the mask was too big for me and it moved everywhere, I took it off," he said in an interview with the sports newspaper *Olé* published in 2021. Leo scored two goals and, at halftime, his coach replaced him at the request of . . . his dad! Concerned about his son's attitude, Jorge Messi implored the coach to take him off the field. "At that moment, I didn't realize the danger, what could happen. I wanted to play no matter what." Despite the fleeting performance of their star, Barça won 4-1 and were crowned champions.

IF ONLY

In the U-17 World Cup in Finland in 2003, Argentina lost the semifinal against Spain. Returning to their hotel, the South American team went to the restaurant for dinner. In the middle of the meal, the chef of the Iberian team, which was staying in the same place, approached the Albiceleste coach, Hugo Tocalli, to reprimand him: "If you had brought that kid Messi from FC Barcelona, you would have been champion!"

FC BARCELONA—FIRST TEAM DEBUT

Lionel Messi made his debut with the FC Barcelona first team without ever having trained with the senior squad. The match took place on November 16, 2003, when the Spanish team traveled to Portugal to face the Porto club in a friendly—the Lusitanian side was managed by José Mourinho and won the UEFA Champions League that year. For that match, Dutch coach Frank Rijkaard decided to promote several rising stars from the *culé* youth academy, including *La Pulga*. In fact, Rijkaard and Messi—then only 16 years old—met in person at El Prat airport in the Catalan capital, before leaving for the city located on the banks of the Douro river. Leo, who was on the substitutes' bench, came out onto the pitch at the Estádio do Dragão in the 75th minute, replacing Fernando

Navarro and wearing the number 14 on the shirt. Porto won 2-0. "I had a hard time falling asleep the night before the game. I was so immersed in it that I couldn't close my eyes. I just wanted to play. I could do it and I am very happy," declared Lionel, hours after his debut in the elite *Blaugrana*.

NEXT LEVEL

At the end of 2003, something amazing happened: the FC Barcelona coaches decided to promote Lionel Messi, who was 16 years old, from the boys A team to the FC Barcelona C team. The team was made up of boys between 18 and 21 years old, competing in Group V of the Third Division, the fourth category of Spanish soccer behind La Liga, the Second, and the Second B. Until the addition of The Messiah, FC Barcelona C had won just one game out of 15 and was in the bottom of the table in the relegation zone. But Leo arrived and the team won three games in a row. *La Pulga* played just 10 games with the C team, enough to avoid losing the category: five wins, four draws, and only one defeat. Immediately, Messi went up a level: he went to Barcelona B, which competed in Second B, the third ranking in Iberian soccer. "If in the morning he played with *Barça* B, then he would go to see the youth squad. And if he had played with the youth, he would go to see Barça B. They were all his teams and he had friends in all the locker rooms. He wanted to play, learn, improve, compete and surpass himself every day. He is a born winner, very fast physically but also mentally," described Pere Gratacós, one of his coaches during those years.

MEMORABLE DATE

June 29, 2004, Lionel Messi played his first game with the Argentine shirt. The match was played on the Argentinos Juniors club field between the U-20 teams of Argentina and Paraguay. The game was organized especially so that Leo would be linked to the national team of his country of birth, meaning that he could no longer play for Spain, which wanted him in its ranks. Argentina won 8-0 and *La Pulga*, wearing shirt 17, scored the seventh local goal.

LEONARDO

The arrival of Lionel Messi in the Argentine national team took place amid endless questions. A few months after the coach of the U-17 team, Hugo Tocalli, was warned by the Spanish chef in Finland, alarm bells went off in the Argentine Football Association (AFA): someone in Europe warned that the Spanish Federation had tried to tempt the little Rosario player to dress in red. Although Leo's desire was to play for Argentina, joining the Iberian squad was tempting, as several of his friends from FC Barcelona trained there. To avoid the loss of the star that everyone was talking about, but almost no one knew in Argentina, Tocalli asked Omar Souto, an employee of the AFA training complex, to get him the phone number of "Leonardo" Messi—the full name commonly used in Argentina for those nicknamed Leo. Souto contacted Newell's and River, but no one in these two clubs had links with the young player. "I went to a phone booth in Monte Grande [a town in the south of Greater Buenos Aires]. I asked for a Rosario phone book, because we only knew that he was from Rosario. I ripped out the page where the Messi numbers were, made a random call to my house to justify that I had entered and returned to the AFA training camp to follow the trail of Leo," Souto said in a documentary produced by the *América Televisión* channel. The first relative that the employee managed to contact was the young star's paternal grandmother. The woman gave him the phone number of one of her children, and he, in turn, that of his brother Jorge Messi in Spain. Souto introduced himself as an employee of the AFA National Teams Department, and asked for "Leonardo Messi." "Finally! My son wants to play for the Argentine team!" celebrated Jorge, who immediately clarified: "His name is not Leonardo, but Lionel." But Souto misunderstood and the confusion did not end there: the request that the AFA sent by fax to the FC Barcelona offices before the match against Paraguay required the loan of the player . . . "Leonel Mecci!"

> There were informal contacts with the Spanish squad, but I always said that I wanted to play for my country because I love Argentina and I only feel the colors of my team."
> (Lionel Messi, after realizing his dream: wearing the light blue and white shirt.)

NUMBER 30

Back in Spain, the 2004/05 season was exciting for Lionel Messi. While still a member of the youth division, he played an official match in the Iberian League for the first time, at the age of 17 years, 3 months, and 22 days, a mark that placed him in seventh place among the most precocious players on the *Blaugrana* team. Leo made his official debut against Real Club Deportiu Espanyol in the Catalan derby. Barça won 1-0 with a goal from the Portuguese Deco. Leo replaced the Lusitanian scorer in the 83rd minute, barely coming into contact with the ball. The Argentine wore the number "30" on the back of his shirt—a tribute to Deco's 20 and Brazilian Ronaldinho's 10, who were his idols. *La Pulga* kept the shirt for his mother, who was in Argentina. "I will remember these minutes all my life," he said excitedly to the press after the match.

On October 28, Messi was chosen to start for the first time in a "points" match. The game was equivalent to the Spanish Copa del Rey, against the modest UDA Gramenet, a club from the Second Division B—the third level of Iberian soccer. The *Barça* team lost 1-0 at the Municipal Stadium of Santa Coloma, a small coliseum with capacity for only 5,000 seated spectators, and was eliminated from the competition. In that same field nine months earlier, Messi had scored a hat trick against Gramenet B, playing for Barcelona C in a third division tournament.

TRIBUTE TO CELIA

Every time he scores a goal, Lionel Messi looks at the sky and points his two index fingers upward. He made this gesture to dedicate the achievement to his grandmother, Celia, who died in May 1998 when he was 11 years old. "I think about her a lot. I wish she had been in the stands today, watching me and enjoying," Messi told to the press in 2005, after scoring his first goal in the Spanish League with FC Barcelona.

FATE

Lionel Messi's debut in the European Champions League, the most prestigious continental club competition on the planet, took place on December 7, 2004. FC Barcelona lost its visit to FC Shakhtar Donetsk of Ukraine, 2-0, in the last match of the group stage. The *culé* team, which had already qualified for the round of 16 after a 1-1 against Celtic FC in the Nou Camp, Barcelona, presented a squad made up mainly of substitutes and youth players, with *La Pulga* completing the starting lineup. Lionel Messi's first official goal with the main FC Barcelona team was celebrated on May 1, 2005, in a La Liga match. That day, the Catalan team beat Albacete Balompié 2-0 in Camp Nou in front of 80,000 fans. Messi replaced Cameroonian Samuel Eto'o, scorer of the *Blaugrana's* first goal, in the 87th minute. Sixty seconds later, Leo received a pass from Ronaldinho, launched a subtle lob over visiting goalkeeper Raúl Valbuena, and the ball ended up in the net. This scoring debut for Messi had a degree of fate because Dutch coach Frank Rijkaard had not originally included him among the substitutes. But, in the last practice before facing Albacete, Argentine striker Maxi López fractured the fifth metatarsal of his right foot, which opened a vacancy on the bench, which was occupied by *La Pulga*. That victory consolidated the leadership of FC Barcelona, which would become champion of the Iberian League the following day, drawing as a visitor with Levante Unión Deportiva (1-1) at the Ciutat de València stadium.

NUMBERS

Top scorers in a single club:

Player (Country)	Club	Score
1 Lionel Messi (Argentina)	FC Barcelona (Spain)	672
2 Pelé (Brazil)	Santos (Brazil)	643
3 Gerd Müller (Germany)	Bayern Munich (Germany)	566
Fernando Peyroteo (Portugal)	Sporting Lisboa (Portugal)	544
Josef Bican (Austria)	Slavia Praga (Czech Republic)	534

ULTIMATUM

For the debut against the US in the U-20 World Cup in Holland, June 11, 2005, the Argentine coach Francisco Ferraro made a decision that, over the years, would become inconceivable: he set up the team's attack with three boys who were around 20 years old—Pablo Vitti (from the Rosario Central club), Gustavo Oberman (from Argentinos Juniors), and the offensive midfielder Emiliano Armenteros (from Banfield). On the bench, the coach left a little boy who had not yet turned 18 years of age: Lionel Messi. "The doctor informed me that Lionel had muscle fatigue and that it was best for him to play only the second half," Ferraro apologized when asked about that episode years later. Nobody believed him. Argentina lost 1-0, despite the fact that the star from FC Barcelona played, in effect, the second half. Pressed by the defeat, the coach decided to modify his position and include *La Pulga* from the start in the next game. An unofficial version claims that the president of the AFA, Julio Grondona, threatened to fire Ferraro on the spot if he didn't include Leo in the starting lineup of the next match.

Whether that supposed ultimatum was true or not, Messi started all the remaining games. With the 18th shirt—the "10" had been assigned to a Vélez youth player, Patricio Pérez, who did not intervene for a single second in the contest—Leo led the team to win all the following games decisively: 2-0 against Egypt (Messi scored one of the goals); 1-0 against Germany; 2-1 against Colombia in the round of 16 (the "18" got another); 3-1 against Spain in the quarterfinals (*La Pulga* reached the third, which made suffer the cook of the red squad); 2-1 against Brazil in the semi (The Messiah scored the first); and 2-1 against Nigeria, in the final played at the Galgenwaard stadium in the city of Utrecht, in which the young star scored a double from the penalty spot. Messi not only received the gold champion medal, he also won the Golden Ball for best player and the Golden Boot for top goalscorer, with six goals. Not bad for a simple substitute . . .

FIRST DOUBLE FOR FC BARCELONA

January 29, 2006, at the Estadi de Son Moix in Mallorca, Lionel Messi scores his first double for the main team of FC Barcelona. Notably, Leo was not in the starting lineup—his entry to the field occurred 28 minutes into the second half, replacing the Swede Henrik Larsson. In just eight minutes, La Pulga made two goals that rounded out a final victory for *Barça* by 0-3.

RED CARD

The Ferenc Puskás stadium in Budapest witnessed an unusual premiere. On August 3, 2005, 63 minutes into a friendly between Hungary and Argentina, Lionel Messi made his debut for the Albiceleste senior team. "I'm happy to play for a second," the FC Barcelona kid said a day before. His wish was fulfilled. He played for a second but not much more. The debut of the great soccer player lasted only a minute and a half. Leo entered the field with the number 18 on his shirt, replacing Lisandro

López. He received the first ball from another Lionel (Scaloni, future coach of the Argentine national team) and *La Pulga* returned it to him with a single touch. A few moments later, Messi dominated the ball and outran defender Vilmos Vanczák. The Hungarian grabbed him by the shirt and, in a reflexive act to free himself, Leo threw two swats back. One of the blows grazed Vanczák's neck, and he fell as if he had been pierced by a burst of shrapnel. The German referee Markus Merk bought the Magyar's performance, showing the rookie a direct red card. "It wasn't the debut I dreamed of," the little man from Rosario acknowledged as soon as he left the locker room, his face swollen from tears. Later, at the hotel, the young star, convinced that this had been his debut and farewell, told his roommate, Pablo Zabaleta: "They're not going to call me again." A prediction that, clearly, did not come true.

For me there is no pressure. I just play. I do what I like and I do it the best I can." (Lionel Messi, in his first interview with the Barcelona newspaper Mundo Deportivo in November 2003).

SPANISH CITIZENSHIP

Due to the large number of FC Barcelona players without a European Union passport, including the Brazilians Ronaldinho, Juliano Belletti, Sylvinho, and Thiago Motta, or the Mexican Rafael Márquez, Lionel Messi decided to obtain Spanish citizenship so as not to occupy one of the places allowed by the Federation for foreign players. The ceremony took place on September 26, 2005, in the civil registry building of Barcelona. After Leo swore allegiance to the Spanish Constitution, a *Barça* manager informed the Royal Spanish Federation, by fax, of the Argentine's new status as a community player. Five days later, on October 1, 2005, Messi played without occupying a foreign-player spot. At the Camp Nou, the Argentine player—already wearing number 19, which had been vacated by Fernando Navarro's departure to the Mallorca club—replaced the Frenchman Ludovic Giuly in the 64th minute of the match against Real Zaragoza, which ended 2-2. On October 22, *La Pulga* entered a La Liga match from the start for the first time. At the Camp Nou, FC Barcelona beat Osasuna, 3-0. Leo played the 90 minutes and, although he did not score, he was named the star of the match by the newspaper *Mundo Deportivo.*

DID YOU KNOW?

Lionel Messi's official debut with the Argentine shirt took place on September 3, 2005, at the Defensores del Chaco stadium in the city of Asunción, in a match equivalent to the Qualifiers for the 2006 World Cup in Germany. Leo entered at 80 minutes and failed to reverse a 1-0 defeat against the local team, Paraguay.

MAGIC

From the victory against Osasuna, Dutch coach Frank Rijkaard decided to give more minutes to Lionel Messi, so that he could add his magic to the powerful offensive trident made up of Ronaldinho, Eto'o, and Deco. Thus, FC Barcelona put together a string of 14 consecutive victories, in which *La Pulga* was in the starting line up in nine and came on as a substitute in four. Furthermore, the *culé* team swept the first phase of the European Champions League: five wins and one draw, against the Greek club Panathinaikos in Athens. At the Camp Nou, *Barça* thrashed the Hellenic squad, and Leo scored his first goal in the Champions League on November 2, 2005. Messi's effectiveness extended to the first leg of the round of 16 of the European tournament, where, on February 22, 2006, against the English club Chelsea in London, the Barça team won 1-2. According to *Mundo Deportivo*, the Argentine was the hero of the match: "Prodigious. He is a phenomenon and adds to his excellent technique a bravery that makes him not hide when they brazenly go after him. His match was one to frame. World consecration."

A LEADER

The second leg against Chelsea, in the round of 16 of the Champions League, on March 7, started very badly for Lionel Messi: 20 minutes into the match, he felt a sudden 'pop' on the inside of his right thigh. The Argentine star tried to continue on the field, but he wasn't able to run due to the discomfort. Distraught, Leo asked to be replaced. Afterward, he cried about his bad luck in the locker room. "Messi suffered a strain in the hamstring muscles of his right leg against Chelsea," which caused "a five-centimeter fibrillar tear in the biceps of his right leg," the club officially reported. The team doctor, Lluís Til, specified that "it is an injury typical of sprinters, of players who start very quickly and make changes of pace." *La Pulga* missed 17 games at the end of the season, in which *Barça* won the Spanish League and also the Champions League. Although he could not play because of his injury, Lionel Messi traveled with the squad to Paris to watch the final against the London club Arsenal. After a 2-1 victory at the Stade de France in the French capital, the Catalan team returned on a charter flight to its city of origin. In the middle of the celebrations, the players and coaching staff were surprised when Leo, until then always shy and laconic, took a microphone and, euphoric on behalf of his teammates, demanded that the club president, Joan Laporta, would reward the conquest with . . . an apartment for each player! "*Presi*, enough of the watches! We want an apartment for each one, we don't want any more watches." *La Pulga's* amazing attitude not only sparked laughter among the plane's passengers but the players discovered that a leader was beginning to mature within that daring boy.

MEMORABLE DATE

October 9, 2005: Lionel Messi played his first game in the starting line up with the Argentine national team. On River Plate's field, the Albiceleste squad defeated Peru 2-0 in a match corresponding to the South American Qualifiers for the 2006 World Cup in Germany.

ON THE BENCH

Lionel Messi recovered in time from hamstring injury to join the Argentine team in the 2006 World Cup in Germany. The delegation stayed at the Herzogspark hotel in the city of Herzogenaurach, located on the outskirts of Nuremberg. There, the squad trained at the Adi-Dassler-Sportplatz complex, named in honor of the founder of the *adidas* company, the sponsoring company of *La Pulga* and also of the South American team. Argentina started the World Cup with a solid 2-1 victory over Ivory Coast, at the Volksparkstadion in Hamburg. Coach José Pekerman left Messi and Carlos Tevez, at that time star of the Brazilian club Corinthians, on the bench. "Rarely did Argentina have the luxury of having such valuable elements as Carlos Tevez and Lionel Messi available and not using them," complained the Buenos Aires newspaper *La Nación*.

We should not go at the speed that people or the press expect because, if something goes wrong, the only one who will be harmed will be the kid. And Messi is that, just a kid. Today he may be a little frustrated, but tomorrow he will be okay. He's in a group that loves him and accepts him. He still has the World Cup to play in."

(Argentine coach José Pekerman, when justifying why he did not include *La Pulga* in the team that debuted in the 2006 World Cup in Germany.)

THE FINAL GOAL

On June 16, in the Gelsenkirchen stadium, Lionel Messi's opportunity at the World Cup finally arrived. In the second game, against Serbia and Montenegro, Leo replaced Maximiliano Rodríguez in the 75th minute. At that moment, Argentina was 3-0 up on the scoreboard. The South

American team finally won 6-0, with *La Pulga* scoring the final goal. At 18 years and 357 days old, Messi became the youngest Argentine player to debut (and, logically, to score) in the World Cup, and the sixth youngest to score a goal. Then, in Qatar 2022, the Spanish Pablo Gavi Páez would sneak into third place, relegating Leo to seventh position.

DID YOU KNOW?

The quarterfinal match of the 2006 World Cup in Germany between Argentina and Mexico was played on June 24, the day Lionel Messi turned 19 years old. Leo was not in the starting lineup but came on in the 84th minute to replace Javier Saviola. That was not the only celebrations that day for the Albiceleste team: Juan Riquelme, also born on June 24, but in 1978, blew out 28 candles. He played play the entire match—which Argentina won 2-1 in extra time.

WATCHING HELPLESSLY

In the quarterfinals of Germany 2006, the Argentine squad faced the host team and favorite for the title—having won four in a row—at the Olympiastadion in Berlin. Coach José Pekerman assembled a line up without Lionel Messi, who was confined to the substitute bench. Argentina opened the scoring in the 49th minute with a header from Roberto Ayala. In the second half, Pekerman exhausted the three substitutions without *La Pulga*, the ideal player to lead a counterattack. Germany equalized 10 minutes before the end, with a goal from Miroslav Klose, and after extra time passed without further goals, the local team won the tiebreaker with shots from the penalty spot. Local goalkeeper Jens Lehmann saved two shots by Ayala and Esteban Cambiasso. Leo was left fuming over the Albiceleste's elimination, watching from the substitute bench. "The impotence I felt for not being able to help the team bothered me," Messi admitted. "I was upset in the extra time because I couldn't do anything to assist my teammates," he added.

NUMBERS

Youngest players to score to score a goal in the World Cup:

Player	Country	Age	World Cup
Pelé	Brazil	17 years and 239 days	Sweden 1958
Manuel Rosas	Mexico	18 years and 93 days	Uruguay 1930
Pablo Gavi Páez	Spain	18 years and 110 days	Qatar 2022
Michael Owen	England	18 years and 191 days	France 1998
Nicolae Kovács	Romania	18 years and 198 days	Uruguay 1930
Dmitri Sychey	Russia	18 years and 232 days	Korea-Japan 2002
Lionel Messi	Argentina	18 years and 357 days	Germany 2006

The 2006/07 season marked Lionel Messi's consolidation into FC Barcelona's first squad. Leo was in the starting line up from the first match and the **culé** team delivered strong performances in both the Spanish league and the European Champions League. A new double appeared on the horizon. However, on match day 10, against Real Zaragoza, *La Pulga* received a strong blow from skilled defender Alberto Zapater that caused a fracture in the fifth metatarsal bone of his left foot. Messi underwent surgery at the Asepeyo Hospital in Sant Cugat. The traumatologist in charge of the intervention, Dr Antoni Dalmau, reported that he placed a 5-centimeter screw to stabilize the affected area "more safely," and that he performed a skin graft to "speed up recovery." Due to the injury, Leo missed 18 games of the season, including 11 in La Liga, 2 in the Champions League, and the Club World Cup in Japan, in which Barcelona lost 1-0 to Internacional from Brazil.

HAT TRICK

March 10, 2007: Lionel Messi scored his first hat trick in a La Liga match. At Camp Nou, Leo scored three times against Real Madrid. The great Spanish classic ended 3-3.

DRAMA

The 2006/07 Spanish League ended dramatically: Real Madrid and FC Barcelona finished level on 76 points. However, the championship went to the team from the Iberian capital: the rules of the competition state that, when the teams are tied, the head-to-head record between them serves as the first tiebreaker. As the *Merengue* team had won 2-0 in Madrid and tied 3-3 at the Camp Nou, they were crowned the winners. The Barça squad had already been eliminated from the Champions League in the round of 16 against the English club Liverpool, so Lionel Messi's disappointment was doubled—or tripled—because another unexpected situation occurred in the semifinals of the Copa del Rey: Barcelona beat Getafe 5-2 in the "first leg" match, at home and with two goals scored by The Messiah. One of the goals was almost identical to the legendary strike from Diego Maradona against England in the 1986 World Cup in Mexico: Leo picked up the ball in his own half on the right wing, slipped past defenders—nutmegging one,—and ran at full speed toward the Getafe penalty area. Evading two more opponents, then the goalkeeper, he scored with his right foot over the body of a defender. Great goal! But, for the second leg, Dutch coach Frank Rijkaard opted to leave Messi resting at home and bring some substitutes to the Coliseum Stadium in Getafe: the home team won 4-0 and eliminated the *Barça* squad.

COPA AMÉRICA

The Copa América held in Venezuela between June and July 2007 left a bitter taste in Lionel Messi's mouth for the fourth consecutive time. Leo joined the Albiceleste squad as an immovable starter in the offensive sector of the field. The team, led by Alfio Basile, won five consecutive games: 4-1 against the US, 4-2 against Colombia, 1-0 against Paraguay (all three, in the group stage), 4-0 against Peru (quarterfinals), and 3-0 to Mexico (semi). *La Pulga* scored two goals in the last two games. In the final, Argentina was widely surpassed by Brazil, which became champion after defeating its classic rival with an unappealable 3-0.

The best in the world is Messi, and the second best is an injured Messi."

(The former Argentine soccer player and coach Jorge Valdano, in an interview given to RAC1 radio in Barcelona in November 2013.)

COINCIDENCE

Lionel Messi not only copied Diego Maradona's second goal against England in Mexico 1986 in that Copa del Rey game versus Getafe, a few months earlier, against RCD Espanyol, Leo copied the first of Diego's goals against the British team, also memorable: the "Hand of God." The striking coincidence occurred at the Camp Nou stadium on June 9, 2007. Like Maradona, *La Pulga* entered the area to look for a bad clearance from a defender and anticipated the Cameroonian goalkeeper Carlos Kameni with his left hand. As had happened with Maradona in the World Cup, neither the referee nor the linesman noticed the mischievous maneuver, so the goal was credited.

A NEW ERA

"Like the rest of my teammates, I want to redeem myself from the last season. I haven't forgotten it," Lionel Messi told *Mundo Deportivo* hours before the start of the 2007/08 competitive calendar. Despite Leo's optimism, FC Barcelona's performance was disappointing for the fans and, of course, for the players: they finished in third place in the local League table, lost in the semifinal of the Copa del Rey against Valencia, and in the Champions League, they were eliminated in the semifinals by Cristiano Ronaldo's Manchester United, who would later become champions. *La Pulga*, despite a new injury that sidelined him for several games (a tear in the femoral biceps of his left leg), improved his numbers: he played in 40 matches, more than in the three previous seasons, and consolidated his emerging leadership with his first goal from the penalty spot in an official *Blaugrana* match, in the absence of the designated penalty taker, the Brazilian Ronaldinho, against Sevilla on September 22. The inconsistent performance of the *culé* team put an end to Frank Rijkaard's time in charge, opening the door to a period that would be historic for world soccer: the era of Pep Guardiola.

OLYMPIC GOLD

In August 2008, Lionel Messi hung a very special award around his neck: the Olympic gold medal. Authorized by FC Barcelona and his new coach, Josep Guardiola, Leo traveled to China to compete in the Beijing Games with the Argentine Under-23 team. The Albiceleste squad won all its games: 2-1 against Ivory Coast, 1-0 against Australia, and 2-0 against Serbia in the group stage; 2-1 to the Netherlands in the quarterfinals; 3-0 to Brazil in the semifinal; and 1-0 to Nigeria in the final, with a goal scored by *Fideo* Ángel di María. *La Pulga* scored two goals: one against the Ivorians, another against the Dutch team. In the semifinal, Messi faced one of his idols and his former teammate at Barça: Ronaldinho, who had to settle for the bronze medal.

MESSI V RONALDO

April 23, 2008: For the first time, Lionel Messi and Cristiano Ronaldo faced each other on the field. The match between FC Barcelona and the English club Manchester United, the first semifinal of the 2007/8 European Champions League, was played at Camp Nou and ended without goals. The Portuguese striker took a penalty, but his shot went high and wide.

JOSEP PEP GUARDIOLA

The arrival of Josep *Pep* Guardiola revolutionized FC Barcelona, not only because of the quality of the performance in each match and the number of titles won by the Catalan squad under his command but also because the young manager's team cemented Lionel Messi as the best player of his time. For the 2008/09 season, the brand-new coach replaced the departures of established players, such as Ronaldinho and Deco, with a structure that at that time didn't seem as good in terms of names—such as the Spanish Andrés Iniesta and Xavi Hernández, or the Ivorian Yaya Touré, for example—but it worked perfectly, like a well-calibrated machine. In just one year of competition, *Barça* won the Spanish First Division tournament, the European Champions League, and the Copa del Rey. "Guardiola made us grow as a team," Leo admitted in November 2022 during a talk in the *Universo Valdano space on Movistar Plus+*. "He taught me how to grow. He always looks for the best for his players. He is very important to me," he added in an interview with the newspaper *Olé*. According to the book *Herr Pep*, by journalist Martí Perarnau, Guardiola summoned *La Pulga* to his office one night. There, he showed him videos with edited images of Real Madrid's defensive movement and he pointed out to Leo the gap that the team—then coached by Juande Ramos—was leaving in its defensive line. "It is better to arrive in the area than to be there," commented the coach in that unusual meeting, in which he added that "the best players go through the center." Guardiola proposed that the Argentine player change his position on the playing field, from the right wing to attacking midfielder. The new feature, which was dubbed “false 9”, allowed Messi to double his effectiveness at the goal. But Pep, modest, never took responsibility for the success of his star. During a conference in Buenos Aires in 2013, he stated that “we have won a lot at Barcelona, but the truth is that we would not have won as much without Leo. You can control some things, but a ball arrives and he, surrounded by four, put the ball at an angle. What influence do I have in all that? Definitely, his parents made him good.”

The player who does not associate well with Leo Messi is not good for soccer.”
(Statements by former player and current coach Xavi Hernández, published by Mundo Deportivo in January 2015.)

In February 2009, Lionel Messi was coached for the first time by Diego Maradona, who a few months earlier had been appointed manager of the Argentine national team. The match took place in Marseille, where the Albiceleste squad played a friendly against France: Argentina won 0-2 and one of the goals, the second, was scored by the talented FC Barcelona player. But the most striking thing about that “clash of the titans” occurred the day before the match, when the South American team visited the Velodrome stadium, the scene of the international friendly. After the game, some of the players stayed to practice free kicks with goalkeeper Juan Pablo Carrizo. Leo’s turn came: he placed the ball 2 meters outside the area and kicked it with his left foot, looking for the right corner. The shot went very high and wide. Messi turned and began to walk toward the locker room, but Diego stopped him with his loud voice: “Come, *Leíto*.” The coach asked for a ball and put it in the same place from which Messi had shot at the goal.

You're rushing too much, daddy. When you get to the ball, don't take your foot off too quickly. Accompany it more because, if not, it doesn't know what you want it to do, or where you want it to go.

While he gave his explanation, Diego ran two or three steps.

You have to do this, look!

Maradona ran toward the ball and took a lethal left foot shot—the ball hit the net powerfully, 2 centimeters from the junction between the right post and the crossbar. Carrizo flew, but he was unable to deflect the missile.

You see? That's how you have to do it. Accompany it more.

It was a master class from a great teacher to his eager student. Leo learned his lesson and, from that day on, his free kick goal average increased exponentially.

UNEXPECTED ATTENTION

During the 2007 Copa América in Venezuela, the talented Lionel Messi attracted a flood of female admirers. How could such an unusual event occur? In the quarterfinals, Argentina defeated Peru 4-1 at the Metropolitan stadium in the city of Barquisimeto. While the Albiceleste team left the field victorious, once the match was over, a young woman could not contain her euphoria and launched herself from the stalls onto the grass to hug Messi. The girl misjudged her fall from about 4 meters high, and she collapsed at *La Pulga's* feet. Surprised, Leo stopped his walk toward the locker room, helped the young girl up, hugged her, and continued walking. The fan was ecstatic, swearing eternal devotion to the talented player. Enthralled by the charm of the left-handed star, the intrepid young lady did not even notice that two police officers were taking her into custody, trailing her. Love was stronger.

TOP SCORER

The first title of the 2008/09 season won by FC Barcelona was the Copa del Rey. Led by Lionel Messi, the *Blaugrana* squad comfortably beat each challenge—first Benidorm, then Atlético Madrid, Espanyol, and Mallorca—until reaching the final against Athletic Club de Bilbao, which they won comfortably at the Mestalla stadium in Valencia: 4-1. Leo scored the second goal, becoming the top scorer of the competition, with six goals.

NUMBERS

Players with the most minutes achieved in the World Cup:

Player	Country	Minutes
Lionel Messi	Argentina	2,314
Paolo Maldini	Italy	2,220
Lothar Matthäus	Germany	2,045
Uwe Seeler	Germany	1,980
Javier Masherano	Argentina	1,950

UNBEATABLE

The 2008/09 Spanish League started badly for FC Barcelona: first, an exhausted Lionel Messi—fresh from the Chinese Olympic Games and new owner of the *Barça* shirt number 10—could do little to avoid a 1-0 defeat on the field of the modest Numancia club. A week later, the *Blaugrana* team barely managed to draw at home against Real Racing Club de Santander. But from then on, the team led by Pep Guardiola became unbeatable, achieving nine consecutive victories—the Argentine player scored six goals—which placed it at the top of the standings. After a draw against Getafe, Barça won 10 more consecutive victories, with another nine goals scored by *La Pulga*. The Catalan club became unreachable on match day 34 when, at the Santiago Bernabéu stadium in the Spanish capital, they beat their main rival, Real Madrid, 2-6, with a brace and a memorable performance by Leo. The title was secured on May 16, when the *Blaugrana* squad still had three games left to complete its league calendar. Messi's authority was reflected in the fact that he scored six goals against five of the team's rivals: Sporting Gijón (game 3), Atlético Madrid (6), Valladolid (10), Málaga (28), and Real Madrid (34). Lionel, meanwhile, achieved his highest league goal record since his debut in the first team: 23.

100 MATCHES

March 1, 2009: Lionel Messi becomes the youngest *Barça* player in history to reach 100 matches in the First Division—at 21 years and 250 days, Leo surpassed his compatriot Javier Saviola, former holder of that record with 22 years and 129 days.

A HISTORIC SEASON

In the 2008/09 European Champions League, FC Barcelona repeated its overwhelming march shown in the two Spanish tournaments. After beating the Polish club Wisla Krakow in the third qualifying round, the Catalan team easily took first place in Group C, which it shared with Sporting Lisbon of Portugal, Shakhtar Donetsk of Ukraine, and Basel of Switzerland. Then, they defeated Olympique Lyonnais of France in the round of 16 (1-1 and 5-2), Bayern München of Germany in the quarterfinals (4-0 and 1-1), and endured a tough battle against the London team Chelsea FC in the semifinal. The first leg, at Camp Nou, ended with a no-score draw. In the second, Andrés Iniesta scored the decisive equalizer (1-1, when away goals carried extra weight) in the 92nd minute—after a perfect assist from Lionel Messi—while the Spanish team was playing with a man down following the send-off of Frenchman Eric Abidal. In the final, Barça took its revenge against Manchester United at the Stadio Olimpico in Rome, on May 27, winning 2-0 (Leo scored the second, with a header—a rarity for him) and lifted the European Cup. With nine goals, *La Pulga* established himself as the competition's top scorer. FC Barcelona finished off a historic season with the triple crown: Spanish League, Copa del Rey, and Champions League—all in just two weeks.

If Messi played as a goalkeeper, he would score 25 goals per season."
(Thiago Alcântara, Spanish-Brazilian midfielder who was Leo's teammate at FC Barcelona, in an interview with the English newspaper *The Guardian*, in May 2015.)

VICTORY PARADE

After the wonderful victory in Rome, which rounded off a perfect season, the FC Barcelona squad arrived at El Prat airport, got on a bus, and paraded through the streets, including Ronda Litoral, on an open-top bus. The three trophies won in just two weeks took pride of place: the Copa del Rey, the La Liga trophy, and La Orejona from the Champions League. The vehicle crossed the ancient city overwhelmed by millions of fans dressed in Barça shirts and carrying flags and photos of their idols, who covered the streets for 8 kilometers to greet their heroes. The tour ended at the Camp Nou, where 85,000 fans celebrated with the players. During the party, a microphone was passed between the players so that each one could express their joy. Lionel Messi was encouraged to practice his rudimentary Catalan: *"Thank you all. Visca el Barça i Visca Catalunya!"* ("Long live *Barça* and long live Catalonia!"). Once the round was completed, and before the celebration was over, Leo asked for the microphone once again to pay tribute to one of his teammates, the Argentine Gabriel Milito, who had missed the season due to a serious injury to his right knee. The defender had traveled with the team to Rome, but upon returning, instead of participating in the celebrations, chose to go home to rest his damaged joint. *La Pulga* did not forget him, and in a generous gesture that revealed his strong friendship, declared to the crowd: "I want to remember one thing: Milito is not here today. He was always by our side supporting us. He had a very difficult year, and he was with us at all times. Therefore, this triumph is thanks to him too."

GOAL!

During 2009, FC Barcelona won six titles: the Spanish League, European Champions League, Copa del Rey, FIFA Club World Cup, Spanish Super Cup, and European Super Cup. Lionel Messi scored momentous goals in all of those tournaments, except the European Super Cup, which consisted of a single match against Ukrainian club Shakhtar Donetsk. However, he still played his part because he assisted Pedro Rodríguez to score the only goal of that game.

ANTONELA ROCCUZZO

On Sunday, January 25, 2009, Lionel Messi agreed to be interviewed in the studio of the *Hat Trick Barça* program on the Catalan television channel TV3. The report included pre-recorded questions from fans, and one boy asked Leo if he had a girlfriend. "Yes, I have a girlfriend. She is in Argentina. I'm fine," the Argentine star answered concisely. For the first time, La Pulga admitted in public that he was in a formal relationship with Antonela Roccuzzo. Lionel and Antonela had met when they were children through Lucas Scaglia, her cousin and Messi's teammate at Newell's. One afternoon, Lucas invited Lionel to play PlayStation at his house and, shortly after, Antonela arrived to visit her family. The crush was overwhelming . . . and mutual. It is said that, a few days later, Leo, only nine years old, wrote her a letter in which he predicted: "One day we are going to be boyfriend and girlfriend." The couple met a few times in Rosario, until Lionel left for Barcelona. Years later, Messi learned of the death of Antonela's best friend in a car accident. Lionel got on the first plane from Barcelona to Argentina and arrived in Rosario to support his distraught lover. Leo had to return to Spain immediately, but the tie had already been consolidated. The couple saw each other sporadically until a few months before the 2010 World Cup in South Africa, when she agreed to cross the Atlantic to live with the love of her life.

BALLON D'ORS

Lionel Messi holds the record for the most Ballon d'Ors awarded by *France Football* magazine to the best soccer player during the calendar year, chosen by some 180 renowned sports journalists from around the world (in some seasons, the publication presented the award alongside FIFA, so the vote also included coaches and team captains). Throughout his career, Leo has received the prestigious trophy eight times. *La Pulga* was chosen for the first time in December 2009, after his excellent 2008/09 season at FC Barcelona, winner of the Champions League, the Spanish First Division tournament, and the Copa del Rey, among other titles. In that period, Messi had also been crowned the Champions League's top scorer. His excellent performance earned him 473 votes out of a total of 480, a record percentage for this award. Leo was the eighth Barça player to receive the Ballon d'Or, after the Spanish Luis Suárez, the Dutchman Johan Cruyff, the Bulgarian Hristo Stoichkov, the Brazilians Ronaldo Nazário and Rivaldo Ferreira, the Portuguese Luis Figo, and another Brazilian, Ronaldinho. Lionel's Golden Ball trophies included 2010, 2011, 2012, 2015, 2019, 2021, and 2023.

FIRST BALLON D'OR

December 6, 2009: Lionel Messi received his first Ballon d'Or in Paris, from the director of *France Football*, Denis Chaumier. Leo acknowledged the work of his "colleagues, because without them I would not have been able to achieve it. I also want to thank my family and my people for all the support they gave me during all these years until I got here."

CLUB WORLD CUP

In December 2009, FC Barcelona traveled to Abu Dhabi to participate in the FIFA Club World Cup, in which the winners of continental international tournaments, such as the UEFA Champions League or the South American Copa Libertadores, compete each year. In the semifinal, the European team comfortably beat the Mexican club Atlante 3-1, with a goal from their Messiah. The final, against Estudiantes de La Plata from Argentina at the Sheikh Zayed Stadium, was a real surprise: the South American team opened the scoring in the 36th minute with a precise and vigorous header from Mauro Boselli. Estudiantes defended their advantage with integrity, and *Barça* was only able to equalize in the 88th minute with a goal by Pedro Rodríguez. And, in extra time, in the 109th minute, Lionel Messi, evading two defenders, hit a Dani Alves cross . . . with his chest! The ball shot with unexpected power toward the net, unstoppable by goalkeeper Damián Albil. Barcelona won the Club World Cup thanks to its shining star, who scored in a final for the fourth time that year—in addition to the Copa del Rey and the Champions League, he had also scored (twice) against Athletic Club in the Spanish Super Cup in August 2009.

There are times when I would like to go unnoticed, walk down the street calmly."

(Lionel Messi, during an interview given to the Argentine television channel *TyC Sports* in 2013.)

SPANISH LEAGUE

FC Barcelona dominated the Spanish League in the 2009/10 season. The Catalan club won 31 games, drew six, and only lost one, against Atlético de Madrid in the Iberian capital. For the first time, Lionel Messi was crowned the competition's top scorer, with 34 goals in 35 games. Leo scored two hat tricks against Tenerife and Zaragoza, in both cases as visitors, and in the round of 16 of the European Champions League, he was orchestrated all four goals in a 4-0 in victory against the German club Stuttgart. Although *La Pulga* was the top scorer of the tournament with eight goals, the Catalan team could not repeat its European success: in the semifinals, the team was eliminated by Internazionale de Milan, who later became champions. In the Copa del Rey, meanwhile, *Barça* stumbled against Sevilla FC, falling in the round of 16.

CAPTAIN

Lionel Messi was captain of the Argentine national team for the first time during the 2010 World Cup in South Africa in the group stage match against Greece. Leo put on the captain's armband at the suggestion of coach Diego Maradona, who had given the regular captain, Javier Mascherano, a rest in that match. *La Pulga* thus became the youngest captain of the Argentine team in a World Cup, at 22 and 363 days old. Very close to the all-time record: in the 1950 Brazil Cup, the American Harry Keough was the captain of his team against Spain at the age of 22 years and 223 days.

DISAPPOINTMENT

The 2010 World Cup in South Africa meant a new disappointment for Lionel Messi. The Argentine team, led by Diego Maradona, won all of its matches in the first phase, against Nigeria (1-0), South Korea (4-1), and Greece (2-0). In the round of 16, Argentina beat Mexico 3-1. In the quarterfinals, the Albiceleste squad fell heavily to Germany, 4-0. Leo, wearing the number 10 jersey for the first time in the World Cup, said goodbye to the African tournament without scoring a single goal, something that would never happen again in the sport's biggest international competition. He did get an assist, however, for setting up Carlos Tevez in the first goal against Mexico.

NUMBERS

Top winners of the Ballon d'Or for best player of the year:

Player (Country)	Awards	Years
Lionel Messi (Argentina)	8	2009, 2010, 2011, 2012, 2015, 2019, 2021, 2023
Cristiano Ronaldo (Portugal)	5	2008, 2013, 2014, 2016, 2017
Michel Platini (France)	3	1983, 1984, 1985
John Cruyff (Netherlands)	3	1971, 1973, 1974
Franz Beckenbauer (Germany)	2	1972, 1976
Ronaldo Nazário (Brazil)	2	1997, 2002

INJURY

After the World Cup in South Africa, Lionel Messi delivered an outstanding performance in the 2010/11 season: he led FC Barcelona to win the third consecutive Spanish League title and another European Champions League victory. In the local competition, Leo participated in 33 games, scoring 31 goals and recording 18 assists. FC Barcelona also broke the record for consecutive victories in Spain's First Division competition: 16, between October 16, 2010 (a 2-1 win against Valencia) and February 12, 2011 (a draw away to Sporting Gijón). Meanwhile, in the European tournament, *La Pulga* scored 12 goals and 3 assists in the 13 games played by the red and blue squad. Barça was very close to repeating the "triple crown," but it lost the Copa del Rey final against Real Madrid, 0-1 in extra time.

Messi's outstanding performance could have been cut short at the very beginning of the season: on the third round of La Liga, on September 19, 2010, against Atlético Madrid at the Vicente Calderón stadium, *La Pulga* received a tremendous blow to his right ankle from Czech defender Tomaš Ujfaluši. The aggressor received a straight red card, while Messi left the pitch on a stretcher. An MRI determined that Leo did not have a fracture as feared, but rather a sprain of the internal and external ligaments of his right ankle. The Argentine star remained off the field for only ten days: he returned to the team on the 29th, although as a substitute, against the Russian FC Rubin Kazan in the Champions League.

SECOND BALLON D'OR

January 10, 2011: Lionel Messi won his second Ballon d'Or, for the first time awarded jointly by *France Football* magazine and FIFA. Leo beat two of his FC Barcelona teammates, Andrés Iniesta and Xavi Hernández, who had also been crowned champions with Spain in the 2010 World Cup in South Africa. It was the second time that three players from the same team made up the most-voted shortlist. In 1988, the candidates were the Dutch trio from the Italian club AC Milan Marco, van Basten, Ruud Gullit, and Frank Rijkaard, who had also won the European Championship that year with the Netherlands team.

DONATING SHIRTS FOR CHARITY AUCTION

On September 20, 2010, FC Barcelona arrived at the Power Horse Stadium to face local team UD Almería. Before the start of the game, local midfielder Fabián Vargas showed up in the visiting locker room and asked to speak with Lionel Messi for a few minutes. The Colombian player told *La Pulga* that a series of very heavy rainstorms had caused flooding in several towns in his country and asked if he would give him his shirt to auction. The money raised would be used to help those affected by the storm for food, medicine, and clothing. Leo responded that he would be happy to give him the jersey after the match. *Barça* won by a very large 0-8—three of the goals were the work of the Argentine star. "I left the field so angry and sad that I forgot about it," Vargas recalled in 2019, in an interview with the Bogotá newspaper *El País*. But a few minutes later, the Almería prop man told him that Messi was at the locker room door looking for him. "I came out and there he was with a bag. I remember he told me: 'Look, these are the t-shirts that I was able to collect for you'. I thanked him and hugged him. When I opened the bag, there was his jersey, more those of Xavi, Iniesta, Dani Alves, Piqué, Puyol, Mascherano and Pinto. I will never forget that gesture."

We wouldn't be what we are if we didn't have Leo Messi. We would be a good team, we would win games, but not with this solvency."

(Josep *Pep* Guardiola, during the press conference after the match in which FC Barcelona defeated Atlético Madrid 3-0 with a hat trick from *La Pulga* and a record of 16 consecutive victories in La Liga.)

"GREATNESS"

Between April 27 and May 3, 2011, FC Barcelona and Real Madrid met in a phenomenal semifinal in the European Champions League. A week after the *Merengue* team beat the *Blaugrana* 1-0 at the Mestalla stadium in Valencia, in the final of the Copa del Rey, the Catalan side traveled to the Santiago Bernabéu stadium in Madrid to challenge its classic rival in the first of two matches to determine which of the two Spanish teams would play in the Champions League final. The first match was won by Lionel Messi, who scored two goals in the second half: one from the left foot, another from the right, after evading three defenders. Exultantly, the Catalan newspaper *Mundo Deportivo* opined that "with his two goals, the second a new masterpiece, the greatest genius of the modern era returns to soccer its greatness. This time, Di Stéfano played for *Barça*." In the rematch, a 1-1 tie qualified the *culé* squad for the continental final, held at London's legendary Wembley stadium. FC Barcelona became champion by beating English Manchester United 3-1, with another goal scored by *La Pulga*. Messi, the best player in the competition—and in the world—was also crowned top scorer.

MESSI FOUNDATION

Lionel Messi has established the Leo Messi Foundation, whose priority is to provide support for children and adolescents with serious illnesses or in high-risk situations on an international level. Together with the United Nations International Children's Emergency Fund (UNICEF), the institution helps with various projects aimed at preserving three fundamental ideals: health, education, and sports. Among other things, it financed programs dedicated to treating childhood leukemia, donated respirators during the Covid-19 pandemic, and promoted the development of educational projects in Asia and Africa. Leo's commitment to the boys became unbreakable after a visit by the FC Barcelona squad to a hospital that had an area designated for children with cancer. There, *La Pulga* met a bald girl, with whom he talked and played for a while. The girl's mother thanked Lionel for the beautiful moment they shared, and before Messi left, she told him that her daughter's illness was terminal. Leo went out into the hallway, met a journalist from the newspaper *Mundo Deportivo* named Cristina Cubero, who was covering the visit, hugged her, and cried like a baby on her shoulder for several minutes. Cubero said in a report that Lionel confided to her that he always remembers that experience and that, as a result, he committed to working with associations dedicated to treating pediatric patients with cancer.

THIRD BALLON D'OR

The triumphs of FC Barcelona in Spain and the European Champions League paved the way for the greatest *culé* star, Lionel Messi, to obtain his third Ballon d'Or in a row. On January 10, 2012, Leo equaled the—until then unique—feat of the French star Michel Platini, winner of the prestigious award in 1983, 1984, and 1985. Wearing a lilac velvet tuxedo made exclusively for him by the Italian designers Domenico Dolce and Stefano Gabbana, *La Pulga* declared: "I never dreamed of winning a single Ballon d'Or and I have already won three. It is incredible and a pleasure, although I would never have achieved all this without the magnificent teammates I have."

NEAR MISSES

Many players and coaches, such as the Argentine Marcelo Bielsa or the Spaniard Fernando Torres, have stated that one of the main attractions of soccer is that the best does not always win, and the persistent shadow of injustice over the results gives the spectacle a seductive uncertainty that you don't get in other sports. Lionel Messi is, undeniably, an excellent example that the king must often relinquish his crown. In the 2011/12 season, Leo established himself as the best player and top scorer in the Spanish First Division and the European Champions League. However, he had to settle for second place in the Iberian tournament and watching the continental final on television. In the local tournament, *La Pulga* scored 50 goals in 37 games—the highest number in nearly a century of Iberian soccer since the 1928/29 season—and a goal average of 1.35, surpassed only by four past glories: the Basques Agustín Sauto, Isidoro Lángara, and Telmo Zarra, and the Catalan Mariano Martín. Throughout the Spanish tournament, Leo achieved two four-goal games, six hat tricks, and six doubles. Controversial and provocative, the Portuguese José Mourinho, coach of Real Madrid, that season's Spanish league champion, told the *SIC* network: "Messi scored 50 goals, but they were worthless." *Mou* was possibly still resentful from the Champions League semifinal the previous year, and from the Spanish Super Cup that opened the season, where FC Barcelona came out on top after Leo scored three goals in two games against Real Madrid . . .

Throughout the European Champions League, Messi scored 14 goals in 11 games. In the semifinal, Pep Guardiola's team could not beat the English team Chelsea FC: they lost in London 1-0, and then, in the rematch, after going up 2-1, the Catalan squad took control of the match thanks to a penalty awarded by Turkish referee Cüneyt Çakır. However, Leo's shot bounced off the crossbar and disappeared into the Mediterranean night, showing that . . . he *is* human! It would have been one more goal on his account, and the ticket to the final. But *La Pulga* and his team had to settle for "only" four Olympic laps: one in the Spanish Super Cup; another in the UEFA Super Cup after defeating Porto 2-0 in a single match in Monaco; the third in the Club World Cup played in Japan, in which the *Barça* team crushed Santos of Brazil 4-0 in the final; and the fourth, in the Copa del Rey, where Barcelona beat Athletic Club 3-0 at the Vicente Calderón stadium in Madrid. Throughout the season, Lionel netted 73 goals in 60 games, an absolute record in European soccer. The Argentine star shattered German Gerd Müller's record of 67 goals with the Bayern München shirt in the 1972–73 season.

JOYFUL NEWS

June 2, 2012: Lionel Messi scored one of the goals in Argentina's 4-0 win over Ecuador in the Qualifiers for the 2014 World Cup in Brazil. When celebrating, he took a ball and placed it under his shirt to announce that his wife, Antonela, was pregnant with their first child. Thiago Messi was born exactly five months later.

MILESTONES

Coach Josep Guardiola's period ended after the last game of the 2011/12 cycle. Throughout his management, which spanned four seasons, FC Barcelona won 14 of the 19 official tournaments it participated in: two European Champions Leagues, three Spanish leagues, two Copas del Rey, three local Super Cups, two Continental Super Cups, and two Club World Cups. This impressive run did not stop Lionel Messi's hunger for titles. In the next First Division competition, 2012/13, under the leadership of Francesc *Tito Vilanova*, Pep's former assistant manager, Leo scored 46 goals in 32 games, averaging a cool 1.43 goals per match. *La Pulga's* noteworthy performance—which accounted for almost half the team's total goals—helped FC Barcelona not only win the League title but also securing 100 points, a historical record for the Spanish First Division, equaling Real Madrid's previous season. *Barça* won 32 games (another record, also shared with the *Casa Blanca*), drew four, and lost just two. Another milestone for the Catalan squad was reaching 55 points in the first phase of the tournament. Unfortunately for the *culés* fans, the successes did not transfer to the European Champions League or the Copa del Rey: in both tournaments, *Barça* was eliminated in the semifinals. However, the red and blue squad left Europe with a great achievement: on March 12, 2013, Barcelona defeated the Italian club AC Milan 4-0 in the round of 16 and qualified for the next phase with a 4-2 aggregate score, since they had fallen 2-0 at the San Siro stadium in the Lombard capital. For the first time in the Champions League, a team managed to reverse a two-goal difference in the first leg, without having scored as a visitor. Two of the goals that made this possible were the work of the Argentine star, Lionel Messi.

Today I am the happiest man in the world, my son was born. Thank God for this gift!"

(Lionel Messi posted these touching words on his Facebook social media account after the birth of his eldest son, Thiago, on November 2, 2012.)

GOAL-SCORING STREAK

During the 2012/13 Spanish League, Lionel Messi managed to score goals against all the teams in the competition . . . in 19 consecutive games! His extraordinary streak began on November 11, 2012, at the Son Moix stadium in Mallorca, where Leo scored twice for a 2-4 victory for FC Barcelona. Then, he scored two against Zaragoza, two against Levante, two against Athletic Club de Bilbao, two against Real Betis, two against Atlético de Madrid, one against Real Valladolid, one against RCD Espanyol, one against Málaga, one against Real Sociedad, four against Osasuna, one against Valencia, one against Getafe, two against Granada, one against Sevilla, one against Real Madrid, one against Deportivo de La Coruña, two against Rayo Vallecano, and one against Celta de Vigo—a total of 30 hits to the net in those 19 games. Additionally, he scored a double in six straight games. The fantastic streak was halted after *La Pulga* suffered an injury to his right hamstring in a European Champions League match against the French club PSG, on April 2 at the Parc des Princes. Messi returned to compete in the Iberian First Division after three games, and scored three more goals, one against Athletic Club de Bilbao and two against Real Betis. If we discount the games he didn't play, the goal-scoring streak extends to 21 consecutive appearances. The Argentine star's scoring run came to end on May 12, against Atlético de Madrid, although FC Barcelona won 1-2.

FIVE-GOAL RECORD

Lionel Messi scored five goals against the German club Bayer Leverkusen in the round of 16 in the 2011/2012 European Champions League. The duel, played at the Camp Nou on March 7, 2012, ended 7-1. Leo's score is the highest in the history of the continental competition for a single player, but the record is not exclusive: until the beginning of March 2024, *La Pulga* shared it with 14 other players who also scored five times in a game, among them the Norwegian Erling Haaland, the Brazilian José Altafini, and the German Gerd Müller.

FOURTH CONSECUTIVE BALLON D'OR

On January 7, 2013, French magazine *France Football* and FIFA awarded Lionel Messi his fourth consecutive Ballon d'Or, a milestone that, to this date, remains unequaled in the history of soccer. The Argentine star beat his rivals, the Portugal's Cristiano Ronaldo and the Spain's Andrés Iniesta, his teammate in FC Barcelona. After receiving the trophy at the Kongresshauss in Zürich, Switzerland, Leo thanked his teammates from *Barça* and the Argentine national team, especially Iniesta: "It is an honor to be next to you today and to train and play with you every day." Messi also "especially" dedicated the Ballon d'Or award to his wife Antonela, "and to my son," Thiago, then two months old, "who is the most beautiful thing that God gave me."

NUMBERS

Top winners of the European Golden Boot:

Player (Country)	Golden Boot Awards	Season
Lionel Messi (Argentina)	6	2009-10, 2011-12, 2012-13, 2016-17, 2017-18, 2018-19
Cristian Ronaldo (Portugal)	4	2007-08, 2010-11, 2013-14, 2014-15
Eusébio (Portugal)	2	1967-68, 1972-73
Gerd Müller (Germany)	2	1969-68, 1972-73
Dudu Georgescu (Romania)	2	1974-75, 1976-77
Fernando Gomes (Portugal)	2	1982-83, 1984-85

The 2013/14 season got off to a flying start for FC Barcelona—with a new coach, the Argentine Gerardo Martino, and the inclusion of the Brazilian forward Neymar—but not so much for Lionel Messi: the Argentine player suffered two muscle injuries, one in each thigh, which sidelined him from some matches in the League and the Champions League, and also from the South American Qualifiers for the 2014 World Cup in Brazil. Then, on match day 13, at the Benito Villamarín stadium of the Real Betis club, Leo received a strong tackle by defender José Caro Martínez, resulting in another fibrillar tear that kept him off the field for about two months. Despite brilliant performances—such as the day he scored a hat trick against Real Madrid at the Santiago Bernabéu for a 3-4 *culé* victory in the Spanish league—Messi starred in a season with ups and downs, very concerned about injuries ahead of the World Cup. Without being able to fully rely on their star player, Barça began to give ground to an unexpected local champion, Atlético de Madrid led by the Argentine Diego Simeone, who also eliminated Martino's team in the quarterfinals of the European Champions League. The *Azulgrana* team advanced to the final of the Copa del Rey, where they clashed with Real Madrid, who retained the trophy and left *Barça* empty-handed.

TOP SCORER

March 16, 2014: At Camp Nou, Lionel Messi scored three goals for the Osasuna club and became the top scorer in the history of FC Barcelona. With the hat trick, Leo totaled 371 goals and overtook the Filipino Paulino Alcántara, who had netted 369 official goals between 1911 and 1927.

OUTSMARTING THE OPPOSITION

Lionel Messi came very close to winning his first World Cup with the Argentine team in the Brazilian tournament between June and July 2014. Leo, named Albiceleste captain by coach Alejandro Sabella, was outstanding in the group stage, scoring goals in every match: one against

Bosnia and Herzegovina, another against Iran, and two against Nigeria. In the second round, *La Pulga* didn't score, but his contribution was key for the South American team to reach the final: he provided an assist for Ángel di María in the round of 16, against Switzerland, and led the attacks against Belgium and the Netherlands. In the semifinal against the Orange squad, Leo scored one of the shots from the penalty spot, securing victory for the Albiceleste team. That goal had a curious story behind it: one day before the match, Messi asked goalkeeper Mariano Andújar to accompany him to the one of the training fields because he wanted to practice penalty shots. "I'm always going to kick you up to the left and hard," he warned. Leo took around 40 kicks, all at the same place: many were goals and some were saved. But, when against Holland, *La Pulga* sent the ball to the right of goalkeeper Jasper Cillessen, who threw himself to his left. Messi—convinced that the rival coach Louis van Gaal had sent someone to hide in the hills surrounding the property where the team was staying and spy on the team—had staged a clever ruse with Andújar that later bore precious fruit.

In the final against Germany, Argentina had two very clear opportunities to open the scoring during the 90 minutes—one of them blocked by Messi—but in both cases, the ball went wide. The German team won 1-0 with a goal scored in extra time, at 113 minutes, by Mario Götze. Without lifting the Cup, *La Pulga* was left with the small consolation of being named the best player of the tournament.

For me it is a dream to know what it feels like to be world champion."
(Lionel Messi, speaking to the British magazine *ShortList*, in 2015. Leo would one day experience it, albeit seven years later.)

NUTRITION

Fed up with recurring muscle injuries and episodes of nausea and discomfort that had overwhelmed him during some games—to the point of causing him to vomit on the field—Lionel Messi decided to visit an Italian nutritionist named Giuliano Poser, who had been recommended by Martín Demichelis, one of his teammates during the Brazilian World Cup. Leo traveled to the doctor's office in the town of Sacile, in the Veneto region of northern Italy, where *La Pulga* underwent an analysis known as "applied kinesiology", which analyzed his muscular strength. "Based on the results of this study, I dictate the treatment, which is specific for each person, although the basis is always a good diet," Poser explained during an interview with the newspaper *Mundo Deportivo*. "There is a set of five foods that I define as super fuel: water, good olive oil, whole grains and fresh organic fruits and vegetables, that is, not contaminated with pesticides or herbicides because that does a lot of harm to the body. Nuts and seeds are also very good," indicated the specialist. Poser prepared a special diet for the *Barça* player, which included recommendations such as reducing salt and red meat consumption, avoiding sugar and refined flours, and eating fresh fish several times a week. Messi followed the eating regimen strictly, and the results were as immediate as they were impressive: he lost weight and his muscle tone improved. "I ate badly for many years. One, at 22, 23 or 24 years old, doesn't feel anything. I ate chocolate, *alfajores*, I drank sodas. Now I eat well: fish, meat, salad, vegetables . . . I eat a little bit of everything, but orderly. From time to time I have a glass of wine. There is always a time when it is possible. I noticed the change a lot, especially because of the vomiting: I settled down and it didn't happen anymore," the Argentine star revealed a couple of years later during an interview with the *América* channel broadcast in March 2018. In the 2014/15 season, Leo was not injured: he played in all 38 games in the Spanish League and all 13 in the Champions League. In total, in that period, *La Pulga* participated in 57 games, scored 58 goals, and contributed with 27 assists. An explosive performance fueled by Dr. Poser's super fuel.

JERSEY DISPUTE

Despite the defeat of his team, Bayer Leverkusen, 1-3 at home against FC Barcelona in the first leg of the round of 16 of the European Champions Leaguc, Czech player Michal Kadlec was very happy: not only he had scored a goal against his famous Catalan rival, but at the end of the match, he had exchanged shirts with his idol, Lionel Messi. However, the joy was short-lived. Along with the precious memento, Kadlec received insults from his teammate Manuel Friedrich, who had allegedly agreed to the exchange with the Argentine before the Czech. The dispute was noticed by the fans, who became angry because Kadlec and Friedrich, instead of being upset with the loss, argued over who would get the rival's jersey. The issue was resolved with the intervention of the German club's sporting director, Rudi Völler: in a Solomonic ruling, Völler ordered the players to auction Messi's shirt and donate the money to a charity.

PERFECTION

FC Barcelona's 2014/15 season was perfect. With Lionel Messi in magnificent physical form, completing an attacking trio with the Brazilian Neymar and the Uruguayan Luis Suárez, and under the management of Luis Enrique, the *Barça* squad once again won the treble, as in 2008/09, with the Spanish Liga, the European Champions League, and the Copa del Rey. In the First Division championship, Leo scored 43 goals in 38 games, with an average of 1.13 goals per match. In the continental competition, *La Pulga* scored 10 goals in 13 games, in addition to five assists that allowed the Catalan team to sweep passed Manchester City in the round of 16, PSG in the quarterfinals, Bayern München in the semifinals, and crush Juventus of Italy 3-1 in the final at the Olympic stadium in Berlin, Germany. In the culminating match of the Copa del Rey, Messi scored two more goals that allowed his club to beat Athletic Club de Bilbao 3-1.

DEFEAT

At the start of July 2015, Lionel Messi had to endure new frustration with the Argentine national team, led by former FC Barcelona coach Gerardo Martino: the squad reached the final of the 2015 Copa América in Chile with superb performances, such as a 6-1 victory over Paraguay in the semi. However, the last match, against the local team, ended goalless after two hours of play, between the initial 90 minutes and the 30 minutes of extra time. The duel had to be resolved with penalties: Leo scored his, Argentina's first, but then Gonzalo Higuaín and Éver Banega missed, making Chile the champions. Messi endured his third lost final in which his team failed to score, following defeats against Brazil in the 2007 Copa América (0-3) and against Germany in the 2014 World Cup (0-1).

CONFRONTATION

May 6, 2015: At the Camp Nou stadium, FC Barcelona defeated Bayern München of Germany 3-0 in the first leg of the European Champions League semifinal. It was the first showdown between Lionel Messi and Pep Guardiola, coach of the German team, who had returned to his former home. Leo celebrated with two goals!

PABLO CLOWN AIMAR

One of Lionel Messi's great idols is Pablo *Clown* Aimar, a talented offensive midfielder who played for River Plate (Argentina), Valencia (Spain), and Benfica (Portugal), among other clubs, as well as the Argentinian national team. Leo saw him in action on television during Aimar's stay in River, and was dazzled by the Clown's skill. Aimar and *La Pulga* landed in Spain the same year, 2001, and met for the first time at Camp Nou on December 18, 2004. That day, FC Barcelona and Valencia CF drew 1-1 and at the end of the match, Lionel—who had been on the substitutes' bench but did not play—approached his compatriot on the visiting team and asked to exchange shirts. Pablo agreed and thus both began a budding friendship that was strengthened through training, trips, and matches with the Albiceleste national team, especially during the 2006 World Cup in Germany when the two were part of the South American team.

Messi is an inexplicable phenomenon for Science."
(Uruguayan writer Eduardo Galeano, who died in April 2015, during an interview given to the *Todo Noticias* channel three years before his death.)

DESSERT

A shot into the net launched by Lionel Messi can be seen, heard, felt, shouted, and also tasted. The Argentine's pirouettes inspired pastry chef Jordi Roca to create, in mid-2015, a dessert called "Messi's goal." The dessert is available at the three-star Michelin restaurant El Celler de Can Roca, in the city of Girona. The tasty invention is presented in a container that is shaped like half a soccer ball with a green lattice reminiscent of the grass on the field. Inside, passion fruit cream, caramel, mint and eucalyptus are combined, a mix of flavors that, according to the chef, increases "euphoria and joy." But the curious selection of ingredients does not end there: it also includes "two small mango and mint marshmallows that remind us of the canarinha", the Brazilian national team jersey. Jordi Roca stated that "if it is a dream goal, it must be against Brazil!"

SELFIE

As soon as the final whistle blew when Argentina defeated Jamaica 1-0 at the Sausalito stadium in Viña del Mar, for the group stage of the Copa América in Chile 2015, one of the Caribbean soccer players, striker Deshorn Brown, who had been replaced and was on the substitutes' bench, jumped onto the pitch and ran toward Lionel Messi. Surprised, Leo thought that Brown was approaching him to complain, angry about the result, but he immediately understood what was happening: the Jamaican, who had his cell phone in his hand—he had left it on the bench before the game, unusual during an official meeting—wanted to take a selfie with *La Pulga*. The Argentine "10" agreed, and Brown returned to his locker room happy with his souvenir.

TRIUMPHS

In the 2015/16 season, a well-oiled FC Barcelona repeated their achievements with both the Spanish League and the Copa del Rey titles. From the beginning, the Catalan team took the lead in the First Division tournament with four consecutive victories. But, on September 26, 2015, on the sixth day, the squad lost its greatest star: just three minutes into the match against UD Las Palmas, Leo went for a shot, but his left boot collided with the foot of defender Pedro Bigas. *La Pulga* fell to the grass with severe pain in his left knee. The crash caused a tear his medial collateral ligament, which kept him off the pitch for five league games. Messi returned in time to participate in the great Spanish classic at the Santiago Bernabéu stadium, against Real Madrid: Barça won 0-4. With his knee fully recovered, Leo totaled 26 goals and 16 assists that contributed to FC Barcelona winning the title on the last day against Granada CF.

In the final of the Copa del Rey, the *Blaugrana* squad defeated Sevilla 2-0, but their best performance was in the semifinal, against Valencia: in the first leg at the Camp Nou, the *culé* team won by 7-0 with three goals from Messi and four from the Uruguayan Luis Suárez. In the Club World Cup, held in the Japanese city of Yokohama, *Barça* added another title almost without breaking a sweat: they crushed the Chinese club Guangzhou Evergrande (3-0) in the semifinal and then repeated the hat trick in the final, against River Plate from Argentina. Leo scored one of the goals that resulted in a new title for the Catalan institution.

The only disappointment of the season was in the European Champions League: Barcelona came through the group stage undefeated and, in the round of 16, eliminated the English club Arsenal with a remarkable double performance by Messi, who scored two goals in London (victory 0-2) and one at the Camp Nou (3-1). In the quarterfinals, *Barça* once again fell into the spider's web woven by Diego Simeone's Atlético Madrid: the *culé* squad, which had won the first leg 2-1 at home, was eliminated after losing 2-0 at the Vicente Calderón stadium.

FIFTH BALLON D'OR

Leo had one more award to celebrate because on January 11, 2016, *France Football* and FIFA awarded him the Ballon d'Or for the fifth time. The Argentinian star won the vote over the Portuguese Cristiano Ronaldo and, again, over a teammate of his from FC Barcelona—the Brazilian Neymar.

NUMBERS

Top historical scorers in the Spanish La Liga:

Player	Club	Games	Goals
Lionel Messi	FC Barcelona	520	474
Cristiano Ronaldo	Real Madrid CF	282	311
Telmo Zarra	Athletic Club	277	254
Karim Benzema	Real Madrid CF	439	238
Hugo Sánchez	Three clubs*	347	234

**Real Madrid, Atlético Madrid, and Rayo Vallecano*

RUSSIAN WORLD CUP

Lionel Messi's knee injury, in the game against UD Las Palmas, was felt, and strongly, on the other side of the Atlantic Ocean. The Argentine team, without its main player, started the Qualifiers for the 2018 World Cup in Russia very badly. In its first appearance in this competition, the Albiceleste squad lost for the first time on home soil against Ecuador, 0-2 on River Plate's pitch. Then, the team, led by Gerardo Martino, tied against Paraguay in Asunción (0-0) and against Brazil in Buenos Aires (1-1). In the fourth and final match without its hero, Argentina beat Colombia as a visitor (0-1), although it remained out of the World Cup qualification positions. Leo returned to the team for the double date in March 2016; thanks to the leadership of *La Pulga*, Argentina beat Chile as a visitor (1-2), Bolivia as a local (2-0, with a goal from The Messiah), and the ship straightened its course toward the Russian World Cup.

SECOND CHILD

September 11, 2015: Lionel Messi's second child, Mateo, was born in Barcelona. The next day, Leo traveled with Barça to the Spanish capital to face Atlético de Madrid and scored the second *culé* goal for a vital 1-2 victory.

CRUYFF-STYLE PENALTY

At the beginning of 2016, upon hearing the news that the former FC Barcelona player and Dutch coach Johan Cruyff was seriously ill with lung cancer, Lionel Messi and his Brazilian teammate Neymar decided to pay tribute to him in the first game in which *Barça* had a penalty. The opportunity came on February 14 at the Camp Nou, when referee Alejandro Hernández Hernández awarded a penalty for a foul inside the RC Celta area against the Argentinian star at 3-1. Leo placed the ball on the spot, stepped back and, when Hernández Hernández blew the whistle, he ran toward it. Instead of shooting against the goal, *La Pulga* touched it lightly to the side, so that Ney could score the goal. However, the one who sent the ball into the net was the Uruguayan Luis Suárez, who anticipated his teammate and beat the Galician goalkeeper Sergio Álvarez. The Catalan players celebrated, although Neymar, with a smile, "reproached" his Uruguayan friend for the interference.

Why did Messi, Neymar, and Suárez honor the Dutch star with that colorful procedure? Because Cruyff himself had popularized that move in 1982. On December 5, Johan, wearing the Ajax club shirt, pretended to kick a penalty against the Helmond Sport club's goal, but passed the ball to his Danish teammate Jesper Olsen. Unlike Suárez, Olsen returned the ball to Cruyff, who scored into an empty net. That play—completely valid because the penalty is a "direct free kick," according to the regulations—began to be called a "Cruyff-style penalty" after being repeated by television channels around the world, although the Dutchman was not the first to execute it. The pioneer for this type of tactic was Danny Blanchflower, in a qualifying match for the 1958 World Cup in Sweden, between Northern Ireland and Portugal, played in Belfast on May 1, 1957. Blanchflower placed the ball in front of Lusitanian goalkeeper Carlos António Gomes but, instead of shooting toward the goal, he passed it to his teammate Jimmy McIlroy, who scored the final goal to make it 3-0.

Cruyff was grateful for the tribute: "It's a joy that they remember you after so many years. It's nice, these are the beautiful things that soccer gives," he commented to an Iberian newspaper. The great Dutch player died a month later, on March 24, in Barcelona.

Losing still makes me very bitter, but I know that when I get home I have the comfort of seeing my children."
(Beautiful sentiment from Lionel Messi on the Yahoo Sports website in 2015.)

OUT OF REACH

The Copa América Centenario, played during June 2016 in the US—for the first time, the South American competition was held outside its territory—was another bitter pill for Lionel Messi to swallow. In the first round, against Chile in Santa Clara, California, Leo did not play. After a knock to his lower back during a friendly match, he remained on the substitute bench for 90 minutes, something that hadn't happened since the match against Germany in the 2006 World Cup. Despite his notable absence, the Albiceleste squad—still led by Gerardo Martino— won 2-1. In the second game against Panama at Soldier Field in Chicago, Messi did make an appearance, and how! Lionel replaced Augusto Fernández in the 62nd minute, when the score was narrowly 1-0, and in just 25 minutes, he scored a hat trick as Argentina won with a conclusive 5-0. Captain Messi was just able to start in the quarterfinals, against Venezuela, in Foxborough, Massachusetts. *La Pulga* scored a goal against *La Vinotinto*, and another against the US in the semi, played in the city of Houston. The final, again against Chile, was played on June 26 at MetLife Stadium in New Jersey. The Albiceleste squad had the title within grasp, but it escaped them again. After two hours without a goal, the match was decided by penalties. Unfortunately, Messi shocked the world by sending his shot over the crossbar. After several successful conversions on both sides, the title remained in Chilean hands when goalkeeper Claudio Bravo—Lionel's teammate at *Barça*—stopped Lucas Biglia's shot, and Francisco Silva sealed it with an unstoppable 4-2.

OTHER WORLDLY

After FC Barcelona crushed AS Roma 6-1 at Camp Nou, in a group stage of the European Champions League, with two goals scored by Lionel Messi, the goalkeeper of the Italian squad, Polish Wojciech Szczęsny, declared: "*Barça* is a team from another planet. It is very nice to see them play, I really appreciated what I saw. Although it is sad to lose 6-1, it was a very nice match to watch."

SHOCK ANNOUNCEMENT

Following its setback in the 2016 Copa América Centenario in the US, the Argentine team lost four consecutive finals without scoring a single goal (Copas América 2007, 2015, and 2016, and the 2014 World Cup in Brazil). But the landslide did not stop there: minutes after the Centennial tournament ended, Lionel Messi the press microphones and dropped a bomb: "There are now four finals in which we have to lose, three in a row. It is a shame. We try, we look for it, but it doesn't happen. In the locker room I thought that's it, that the National Team is over for me. After four finals, this is not for me." The reporters, perhaps frozen by the star's brutal honesty, did not react. Before they could blink, Messi himself confirmed the worst news: "Unfortunately I looked for it, it was what I was looking for most, it wasn't given to me . . . I think it's done." One of the stunned journalists barely managed to stammer to ask whether it was a final decision. Leo, visibly depressed, continued: "I think so. It's what I feel now, it's what I think. It's a great sadness what happened to us again. On top of that, I have to miss a penalty. I think it's for the good of everyone." "There are many people who are not satisfied. We are not satisfied with reaching the finals and not winning them either." Messi, compassionate with the disoriented silence of the journalists, continued with his painful speech: "I think it's already a final decision. I already tried a lot to be champion with Argentina. It didn't happen and I'm leaving without being able to achieve it."

AT SEA

A 24-year-old young man swam for half an hour in the Mediterranean Sea to meet Lionel Messi. The unusual situation occurred in July 2016, while Leo and his family were staying onboard a yacht off the coast of Ibiza. Upon learning that the ship *Seven C*, anchored more than a kilometer from Les Salines beach, had been rented by *La Pulga*, the boy put his mobile phone in a plastic bag, started swimming for half an hour until he managed to board the boat, with his idol on board. After talking for a while with Leo, the young man tried to take a photograph, but discovered that his phone had been ruined. Messi, very kindly, asked one of the yacht's employees to take a photo of them with his cell phone, and then send it to the young guy's email address. The player also offered his fan a ride to the coast on a jet ski, but the young man refused and swam back, just as he had arrived. "I lost a phone, but I won a photo with Messi," he celebrated upon returning to the beach. "Leo was very hospitable," he later told the newspaper *Mundo Deportivo*: "The way he spoke and addressed me, it didn't seem like I was with a world star. He was very humble, and both he and his family behaved wonderfully," he related.

MEMORABLE MOMENT

September 13, 2016: FC Barcelona achieved its biggest win in the European Champions League: at Camp Nou, the team defeated the Scottish club Celtic 7-0. Lionel Messi was the main scorer of the night, with three goals.

Messi is a Play Station player. Things that are impossible, he makes them possible."
(The French coach of the English club Arsenal, Arsène Wenger, after FC Barcelona eliminated his team in the quarterfinals of the 2009/2010 European Champions League with . . . four goals from Leo!)

BACK IN CHARGE

Two months after his resignation from the Argentine national team, Lionel Messi changed his mind and rejoined the team for the South American Qualifiers for the 2018 World Cup in Russia. "I see that there are many problems in Argentine soccer and I don't want to create one more. I don't want to cause any damage, I always intended the opposite, to help in everything I could. Many things in Argentine soccer have to be fixed, but I prefer to do it from within and not criticize from outside," said the Argentine left-hander through a release. "Many things went through my mind on the day of the last final and I seriously thought about quitting, but I love my country and this shirt too much," Messi proclaimed. On September 1, he took charge once again and led the team to a 1-0 victory of Uruguay in the city of Mendoza. Who scored the only goal of the match? *La Pulga*. Who else?

UPS AND DOWNS

The 2016/17 season did not end as Lionel Messi and his teammates hoped. In the fifth round of the Spanish League, playing at Camp Nou against Atlético de Madrid, Leo suffered a tear in the adductor of his right thigh, which forced him to miss four games. In that time, FC Barcelona lost valuable points that, at the end of the tournament, relegated it to second place, ahead of Real Madrid. The championship escaped the Catalan club, despite the return of *La Pulga* to the team and scoring 37 goals in 36 games, establishing himself as the top scorer of the competition.

Some consolation came with the Copa del Rey, which FC Barcelona won after defeating Alavés in the final, played at Madrid's Vicente Calderón stadium, 3-1. Leo scored two goals against Athletic Club in the round of 16, one against Real Sociedad in the quarterfinals, one against Atlético de Madrid in the semifinals, and another against Alavés in the final. Fantastic!

In the UEFA Champions League, *Barça* was eliminated in the quarterfinals by the Italian team Juventus, who thus took revenge for the final of the 2014/15 season.

SPORTSMANSHIP

Ernesto Vecchio, coach of Lionel Messi in the children's divisions of Newell's Old Boys, said in 2012 that, during a match, *La Pulga* received the ball from his goalkeeper and advanced from his own half, avoiding rivals. When he reached the penalty area, Leo eluded the goalkeeper, who collided with one of his legs. Noticing that his opponent was holding his face and screaming in pain, Lionel stepped on the ball and, instead of scoring with an empty goal, asked the referee to attend to his opponent.

COMEBACK

The most extraordinary comeback in the entire history of the European Champions League, in a two-legs duel, was by Lionel Messi's FC Barcelona. In the round of 16 during the 2016/17 season, the Catalan club lost 4-0 to PSG in the French capital. The playoff seemed resolved, and then the Iberian squad rose from the grave and, at Camp Nou, scored three goals in 50 minutes: Luis Suárez, after 2 minutes; the Frenchman Layvin Kurzawa with an own-goal at 40; and Leo at 50 through a penalty. At 62, a sharp counterattack by the Uruguayan Edinson Cavani crushed the hopes of the *Blaugrana* fans. Barça had to score three goals in half an hour and the performance on the field did not encourage hope. What's more: a little while after the Parisian goal, the Argentine Ángel di María wasted a real opportunity, face to face with the German goalkeeper Marc-André ter Stegen, to settle things. However, Barcelona closed the gap with two goals by Brazilian Neymar—in the 88th with a free kick and in the 91st with a penalty. The victory came in the 95th minute, in the dying minutes, when Sergi Roberto connected with a lofted cross from Neymar that German goalkeeper Kevin Trapp failed to clear. The 6-5 aggregate score still sends chills through the Catalan stands and nightmares for the timid players who wore the PSG shirt that night.

NUMBERS

Players with the most World Cups played:

Player (Country)	Number of World Cups	World Cup
Antonio Carbajal (Mexico)	5	1950, 1954, 1958, 1962, 1966
Lothar Matthäus (Germany)	5	1982, 1986, 1990, 1994, 1998
Rafael Márquez (Mexico)	5	2002, 2010, 2014, 2018, 2022
Andrés Guardado (Mexico)	5	2006, 2010, 2014, 2018, 2022
Lionel Messi	5	2006, 2010, 2014, 2018, 2022
Cristiano Ronaldo (Portugal)	5	2006, 2010, 2014, 2018, 2022

Note: The Italian Gianluigi Buffon and the Aztec Francisco Guillermo Ochoa Magaña were with their teams in five World Cups, but they did not play in all of them.

100TH DOUBLE

March 19, 2017: In FC Barcelona's 4-2 victory over Valencia CF, Lionel Messi scored two goals marking his 100th double with the Catalan first team. Until that day, Leo had scored twice 69 times in La Liga, 19 in the Champions League, eight in the Copa del Rey, two in the Spanish Super Cup, one in the European Super Cup, and one in the Club World Cup.

WEDDING

Lionel Messi and Antonela Roccuzzo were married on Friday, June 30, 2017, at the City Center complex in Rosario, Argentina. The ceremony was performed by the director of the Santa Fe Civil Registry, Gonzalo Carrillo, and Thiago, the couple's eldest son, was the ring bearer. The witnesses were the brothers of the bride and groom, and there were about 250 guests, among whom were several of Leo's teammates from the Argentine national team and from FC Barcelona, and also some former *Barça* players: Luis Suárez, Xavi Hernández, Sergio Busquets, Carles Puyol, Cesc Fábregas, Samuel Eto'o, Jordi Alba, Neymar, Dani Alves, Sergio Agüero, Ezequiel Lavezzi, Ángel di María and Gonzalo Higuaín, along with Gerard Piqué and his wife at the time, the Colombian singer Shakira. Leo did not forget his colleagues from La Maquina del '87 from Newell's Old Boys, and also invited some of his friends from primary school. The couple specifically requested that their guests not give them gifts and instead make monetary donations to a non-governmental organization (NGO) called *Techo*, dedicated to assisting homeless children. "To transform our joy into an act of solidarity, instead of a gift we ask for a donation," they indicated in the wedding invitations. But, despite the fact that among the 250 guests there were many soccer players with million-dollar salaries, the NGO received a total donation of just . . . €9,500!

I'm embarrassed when I see myself on TV. I don't like seeing myself, or watching repeated matches. I stay with the image that was left in my head during the match."
(Lionel Messi, interviewed by *Fox Sport Radio* in May 2019.)

NEW LEADERSHIP

For the 2017/18 season, Ernesto Valverde replaced Luis Enrique as coach of FC Barcelona. This change seemed to motivate the Barça team: a highly inspired Lionel Messi scored 34 goals in 36 games, which not only established him as the competition's top scorer but also propelled the blue and red team to win the Spanish League with four games to spare and undefeated—losing only the penultimate game, when Leo was absent and with several substitutes, by which point, they were already champions. The victory was cemented on match day 35: Barcelona beat Deportivo de La Coruña in an away game, 2-4, with three goals from its top star. With this new title, *La Pulga* added nine league titles and surpassed his compatriot Alfredo di Stéfano, who had achieved eight with Real Madrid. "It has a lot of merit to win a League without losing any game, it is very difficult. We had difficult moments and we overcame them without knowing defeat. Therefore, we have to value it and celebrate it properly, with all the people," Messi shared with the press.

FC Barcelona also won the Copa del Rey, after beating Real Murcia, Celta de Vigo, Valencia, and Sevilla in the final, held at the Wanda Metropolitano, the new home of Atlético de Madrid, by 5-0. Lionel, of course, got on the scoreboard with a great goal.

The triple crown vanished in the quarterfinals of the UEFA Champions League: on that occasion, the Catalan team was eliminated by the Italian squad AS Roma.

LIFESAVING

The passion that the skilled Lionel Messi arouses throughout the world is remarkable. In 2015, a young Argentine agricultural engineer was kidnapped in Nigeria by a terrorist group. The criminals were about to kill the boy because they believed him to be an American. However, his life was spared after the 28-year-old hostage mentioned a magic word:

"Messi." After the company he worked for paid a ransom, the engineer was finally released safely thanks to the admiration that his African captors had for the "10" of the Spanish club Barcelona and the Argentine national team.

VALIDATION

On November 26, 2017, on match day 13 of the Spanish League, Valencia CF and FC Barcelona tied without goals at the Mestalla stadium. Thirty minutes into the first half, Lionel Messi launched a missile with his left foot, sending it at high speed toward the center of the local goal. Norberto Murara Neto seemed to have it under control, but the ball slipped through the Brazilian goalkeeper's gloves, bounced off the grass, and crossed the goal line by a few centimeters. Murara reacted quickly, threw himself back and, with a swipe of his hand, cleared the ball to the side. Neither the referee Ignacio Iglesias Villanueva nor the lineman on that side, Enrique Ramos Ferreiro, noticed Leo's goal and allowed the match to continue with the score still at zero. Only the following season would the video assistant referee (VAR) come into force, which would have easily resolved the issue and awarded the goal to *La Pulga*. The match ended 1-1, despite the protests of the Barcelona players. The most striking thing about the situation is that, even though the goal was not validated by the referee, the betting house Betfair counted it as scored. Through a press release, the company announced that "Betfair, in a gesture of good will and justice with its clients, will not only pay the benefits to those who bet on the tie, but those who bet on the tie will also receive their prize for Barcelona's victory." In addition, the betting house also paid those who had predicted that Messi would score the first goal of the game, something that—even though it did not count officially—because, according to the Federation record, the Valencian Rodrigo Moreno was listed as the first scorer. However, *La Pulga* achieved the impossible: his goal was validated . . . despite the referee!

ROMAN HEROES

The loss to AS Roma in the quarterfinals of the 2017/18 Champions League was as shocking as the comeback against PSG the previous season. The team, led by Lionel Messi, had comfortably defeated the Italian squad in the first leg at Camp Nou on April 4, 2018, 4-1: two own goals, one from Daniele de Rossi, and another from the Greek Kōnstantinos Manōlas, gave the Iberian squad an advantage, which Gerard Piqué and Luis Suárez extended. The goal by Bosnian Edin Džeko gave some air to the aspirations of the Eternal City team. A week later, in the Italian capital, a Giallorossa blast ended the aspirations of the *culé* fans, with a 3-0 defeat. The most notable thing about the scoreboard was that the three players who scored had already done so in Barcelona: Džeko, De Rossi, and Manōlas—the latter taking revenge for their misfortune on Catalan soil. Thus, Lionel Messi and his teammates were left out of the competition in the quarterfinals for the third consecutive year. "The *Blaugranas* were overwhelmed by a Roma team that was superior from start to finish and completed a historic comeback. Valverde's team was an unrecognizable team last night, which suffered in defense, was imprecise in the center of the field and harmless in attack," said *Mundo Deportivo*. Messi, a few days later, admitted in an interview with the Argentine television channel *TyC Sports*: "We messed up. Because of the lead we had, we thought we were already in the semis." Something else that no one should forget: the Roman hero who sustained the miracle was the Brazilian Alisson Becker.

THIRD CHILD

February 10, 2018: Ciro, the third child of Lionel Messi and Antonela Roccuzzo, was born at the USP Dexeus Hospital in Barcelona. Leo did not travel to Málaga with *Barça*: he opted to stay with his wife, the newborn, and his two other children, Thiago and Mateo.

SAVING THE DAY

The Argentine team came very close to missing out on the 2018 World Cup in Russia. The poor results under Gerardo Martino and later Edgardo Bauza left the squad far from the top of the standings in the playoff zone against a team from Oceania. In June 2017, Jorge Sampaoli, who had led Chile to victory in the Copa América in 2015, took over as coach. For the first time in its history, the Albiceleste team had three different coaches during a World Cup qualifying series. Despite the change of manager, the performance was very weak. Argentina drew with Uruguay in the Centenario of Montevideo (0-0), with Venezuela in the River Plate field (1-1), and with Peru in La Bombonera of Boca Juniors (0-0). The Albiceleste team secured direct qualification on the final match day, defeating Ecuador in Quito 1-3, with a hat trick from the great Leo Messi, the hero of their qualification campaign for the Russian tournament.

Leo Messi has a deep commitment to his team. He is supportive, prudent and respectful: when he scores a goal, he runs to hug his teammates, he is not going to celebrate it with the stands."
(Former coach César Menotti, former coach of the Argentine team that won the 1978 World Cup, in statements to the Catalan radio *La Xarxa*, in November 2012.)

DREAMS SHATTERED

In the 2018 World Cup in Russia, the Argentine team delivered its worst performance since Lionel Messi's debut. The squad, which had reached the quarterfinals in the 2006 German and 2010 South Africa Cups, and had lost the final in Brazil 2014, barely made it past the group stage and was eliminated in the round of 16 against France, 4-3. After drawing against Iceland in the opener (1-1, thanks to Nordic goalkeeper Hannes

Þór Halldórsson who saved a penalty from Leo), the Albiceleste side, led by Jorge Sampaoli, was defeated by Croatia, 3-0, in Nizhny Novgorod. In the final group match in Saint Petersburg, Argentina defeated Nigeria 2-1, with a goal from Lionel Messi. Leo's dream was destroyed at the Kazan Arena, where France crushed his dreams.

DIVORCE

During the 2018 World Cup, a marriage from the Russian city of Chelyabinsk dissolved because of . . . Lionel Messi! In reality, Leo did not personally know the members of the couple, Arsen and Ludmyla. According to the Moscow newspaper *Argumenty i Fakty*, Arsen professed excessive admiration for the talented Argentine player. His wife, perhaps jealous, perhaps a fan of Cristiano Ronaldo, mocked excessively when *La Pulga* missed a penalty against Iceland. When the Albiceleste squad defeated Nigeria with a goal from Messi, Arsen retaliated with strong expletives that offended Ludmyla and ignited a fierce argument that culminated in the civil registry, where Arsen filed for divorce.

MEMORABLE MOMENTS

Lionel Messi's scoring ability was renewed in Barcelona after the adverse performance of the Argentine team in the Russian World Cup. Inspired by receiving the captain's armband, following Andrés Iniesta's departure, Leo displayed a stunning performance in the 2018/19 Spanish League, despite suffering from an unusual injury that kept him off the field for five matches of different competitions: in the match against the Sevilla club, on October 20, 2018, in the ninth round of the championship, *La Pulga* crashed into his compatriot Franco Vázquez and, falling awkwardly, he fractured his right radius. Messi, who had scored one of the team's goals that day and provided an assist for another, was treated by the *Barça* team doctor and immediately taken to the Ciutat Esportiva del Barça for further examinations. FC Barcelona won that night 4-2 and took the lead of the tournament from Sevilla, which they would not relinquish until the end. Leo missed two La Liga games and returned to the team with a hunger. On November 11, he scored a double against Real Betis. The Argentine star achieved two impressive streaks, scoring in eight and five consecutive games, which strengthened the Barça team's progress toward a new title in the local competition. Messi, of course, won the Pichichi Trophy once again, with 36 goals in 34 games.

In the Copa del Rey, FC Barcelona experienced unforgettable days, including a comeback against Sevilla (6-1 at the Camp Nou, after losing 2-1 on Andalusian soil), and a 0-3 victory against Real Madrid in the Santiago Bernabéu, after a goalless draw in Catalonia. However, in the final at the Benito Villamarín stadium in Seville, the *culé* squad fell to Valencia CF 1-2, despite another goal from Leo.

NUMBERS

Players with the most games played in the UEFA Champions League:

Player	Games	Clubs
Cristiano Ronaldo (Portugal)	187	Sporting Lisboa, Manchester United, Real Madrid, Juventus
Iker Casillas (Spain)	181	Real Madrid and FC Porto
Lionel Messi (Argentina)	163	FC Barcelona and PSG
Xavi Hernández (Spain)	157	FC Barcelona
Karim Benzema (France)	152	Olympique Lyonnais and Real Madrid

DISAPPOINTMENT

The 2018/19 UEFA Champions League was a tremendous disappointment for FC Barcelona. Despite having the top scorer of the tournament, Lionel Messi, scorer of a dozen goals in just ten games—he missed two matches due to a fractured radius—the Catalan club once again suffered an unimaginable comeback. After going through the group stage undefeated, beating the French club Olympique Lyonnais with ease in the round of 16 (5-1 on aggregate) and the overcoming the always dangerous Manchester United in the quarterfinals (0-1 in England and 3-0 at Camp Nou, with a double from *La Pulga*), the *Barça* squad suffered serious humiliation in the semifinal. On that occasion, Barcelona beat the British team Liverpool 3-0 at home, with another pair of goals from Leo, but at Anfield Road the illusion of a new continental final was shattered: the English team secured an extraordinary 4-0 victory, with two goals from the Belgian Divock Origi and two from the Dutchman Georginio Wijnaldum, who overcame a heavy disadvantage to reach the final, which Liverpool would go on to win against Tottenham Hotspur in an all-English duel. Unusually, Liverpool's goalkeeper was the same player who, the year before, had played a key role in a similar epic with AS Roma against Barcelona: the Brazilian Alisson Becker. "The dream of Messi and the *culés* was taken away by a painful defeat that will be difficult to overcome," stated the newspaper *Mundo Deportivo.*

SIXTH BALLON D'OR

December 2, 2019: Lionel Messi won his sixth Ballon d'Or, breaking the record of five that he shared with the Portuguese Cristiano Ronaldo. Leo surpassed the Dutchman Virgil van Dijk and Ronaldo himself in the vote.

EARTHQUAKE

The seismologist Jordi Díaz rendered all the scientists and attendees at the Congress of the European Union of Geosciences speechless when, at the beginning of April 2018, at the Austria Vienna Center in the Alpine metropolis, the Catalan researcher announced that Lionel Messi's goals caused . . . earthquakes! The unusual announcement was made after Díaz, a member of the Institut de Ciències de la Terra Jaume Almera, placed a seismometer inside a building in Barcelona located five blocks from the Camp Nou. The scientist analyzed the measurements recorded while the *Blaugrana* team faced the English club Chelsea for the second leg of the round of 16 of the European Champions League, on March 14, 2018, in front of about 100,000 fans. Barça, who had equalized in London, needed to win to advance to the next round. When Leo scored the first goal of the match, three minutes into the first half, the device announced a strong tremor, similar to that of a natural earthquake. "We discovered that there was an earthquake, the result of people jumping out of their seats to celebrate," the scientist explained. That night, Díaz indicated, the device registered a large peak immediately when Messi scored his first goal, and another smaller one after the second, which sealed the 3-0 that qualified the Catalan team.

In the end, when all this is over, what do you take with you? My intention is that, when I retire, I will be remembered for being a good guy."

(Lionel Messi's musings when interviewed by Urbana Play radio in January 2023.)

REFEREES

The 2019 Copa América in Brazil began with a setback for the Argentine team and its captain, Lionel Messi. The Albiceleste squad fell to Colombia, 0-2, in the city of Salvador. In that match, new coach Lionel Scaloni made his official debut. Argentina made its qualification more difficult with a 1-1 draw against Paraguay in the second match in Belo Horizonte, but they finally advanced to the second round after beating Qatar—a team invited by the South American Confederation—2-0. After beating Venezuela in the quarterfinals, 2-0, Argentina lost the semifinal against Brazil, although the match was very even, with some mistakes made by the referees in charge of the VAR. After the game, Leo complained vehemently about the refereeing of Ecuadorian referee Roddy Zambrano, which he considered to be biased. He paid a heavy price for his anger: in the match for third place, when Argentina was already winning 2-0, *La Pulga* collided with Chilean defender Gary Medel. The Chilean, known for his quarrelsome nature, launched a header into Leo's face. Messi puffed out his chest and endured the blow without flinching. The fair-minded Paraguayan referee Mario Díaz de Vivar only showed the red card to . . . the Argentine! An apparent reprimand for the Albiceleste captain for his statements after the match against Brazil. The most striking thing about the case was that, acting with false impartiality, Díaz de Vivar approached the VAR monitor, discovered the origin of the conflict and sent off Medel . . . but he did not revoke Lionel's red card. Thus, Messi suffered the second send-off of his career; this had never happened with FC Barcelona, and it was his second send-off with Argentina after 135 games since his brief debut against Hungary. "We do not have to be part of this corruption, of the lack of respect that was shown to us throughout this Cup. Corruption and the referees do not allow people to enjoy soccer. I leave with my head held high," declared Leo. Argentina defeated Chile 2-1, and *La Pulga*, very angry with the referee's performance, preferred to stay in the locker room and not return to the field to collect his bronze medal.

PICHICHI TROPHY

Lionel Messi holds the record for winning the Spanish Pichichi Trophy the most times, an award given to the top scorer of the season in La Liga. Leo achieved it eight times, two more than the famous Basque forward Telmo Zarra—star of Athletic Club de Bilbao between the 1940s and 1950s—and three more than his compatriot Alfredo di Stéfano, the Iberian Enrique Quini Castro and the Mexican Hugo Sánchez.

LOSSES

FC Barcelona's performance in the 2019/20 season can be divided into two parts: on one hand, the results were disappointing for a team accustomed to doing Olympic laps on all fields, and despite the inclusion of valuable players, such as Antoine Griezmann, the champion with France in the Russian World Cup in 2018. On the other hand, Lionel Messi once again was the top scorer in the Spanish League, with 25 goals in 33 games. But, Leo also improved his own record of assists in a First Division tournament: 21. Despite the contribution of the Argentine star, the *Blaugrana* squad played very poorly. They occupied second place in the standings, five points below champions, Real Madrid. In Copa del Rey, they lost in the quarterfinals to Athletic Club de Bilbao. In the UEFA Champions League, which modified its format after the Covid-19 pandemic and moved the competition to Portugal, the Catalan team suffered its worst defeat in an international competition: 2-8 against the German Bayern München. "*Barça* receives the most lacerating humiliation in its history at the hands of a Bayern that reveals its limitations. The 2-8 is an intolerable and deserved blow that increases the drama after the fiascos in Rome and Liverpool," the newspaper *Mundo Deportivo* mercilessly criticized. The campaign was so disappointing for fans and managers that, for the first time since Leo Messi's debut, setbacks cost two coaches their positions in one season: Ernesto Valverde, who resigned in mid-January 2020, and Enrique *Quique Setién*, expelled after the loss against the German team.

Lionel Messi has been applauded in many stadiums. His outstanding performances have aroused respect and even ovations from his rivals, but rarely anything like the day in which FC Barcelona beat Real Betis 1-4 at the Benito Villamarín stadium, on March 17, 2019, for match day 28 of La Liga. *La Pulga* scored three goals, the last of which was a masterpiece: after a corner kick, Messi received a pass from his Croatian teammate Ivan Rakitić and, 1 meter inside the rival area, he faked a powerful left-footed shot . . . but he launched a precise lob. The ball flew past goalkeeper Pau López, kissed the crossbar, and settled into the net. The masterful definition sent 50,000 local fans to their feet, who not only gave a long ovation, chanting "Messi, Messi", but also effusive displays of praise, raising both arms. That night, Leo was revered at the Betis stadium.

GOAL NUMBER 474

May 16, 2021: Lionel Messi played his last game with the FC Barcelona shirt in an empty Camp Nou due to the pandemic. Leo also scored his last *Barça* goal, number 474 in 17 seasons with the Catalan team.

A PROMISE

The start of the 2020/21 season for FC Barcelona was turbulent: Lionel Messi tried to leave the club. "I suffered a lot in training, in games and in the locker room. Everything became very difficult for me and there came a time when I considered looking for new objectives, new airs," Leo acknowledged during an interview with the *Mundo Deportivo* in September 2020, days before the start of his final chapter with the Catalan club. *La Pulga* had wanted to leave at the end of the previous season—his contract allowed it as long as he notified the club before June 10, 2020. However, tournament delays due to the Covid-19 pandemic complicated things—the final League match was played on July 19, and the Champions League was concluded in August. Leo believed that it would have been irresponsible to make a decision before the fixture was completed, but when it was over, the *Barça* club's lawyers demanded that he strictly comply with his contract. "I'm going to continue at Barcelona and my attitude is not going to change no matter how much I wanted to leave. I'm going to do my best. I always want to win, I'm competitive and I don't like losing anything. I always want the best for the club, for my teammates and for me. There is a new coach and a new idea. I'm staying and I'm going to give my best," he promised. And he kept his promise. *La Pulga* was the top scorer in the Spanish League, with 30 goals.

If Messi decides to leave, then we have to find another name for the club."
(Former FC Barcelona Cameroonian striker Samuel Eto'o, interviewed by the *TyC Sports* channel in Argentina in August 2020.)

GOODBYE

In his final season with the Catalan club, Lionel Messi was unable to restore the glory of past *Barça* eras. His goals could not lift a team lacking both character and ability after the departures of players such as Andrés Iniesta, Xavi Hernández, or Neymar, among others. FC Barcelona finished the Iberian League in third place, behind champion Atlético Madrid and runner-up Real Madrid. In the Champions League, the competition ended very early: in the round of 16, *Barça* was eliminated by PSG, who secured a 1-3 away and drew 1-1 at the Parc des Princes in the French capital. The only joy of the season for Messi and the *Blaugrana* fans came in Copa del Rey: FC Barcelona defeated Athletic Club de Bilbao 4-0 in the final at the La Cartuja stadium in Seville. Leo said goodbye with a double.

TRIBUTE

Four days after the death of Diego Maradona, on November 25, 2020, Lionel Messi scored a goal against CA Osasuna that rounded off a 4-0 victory. After celebrating the conquest with his teammates, Leo took off his blue and red shirt and, underneath, he had one of Newell's Old Boys' shirts that Maradona had worn during his brief time at the Rosario club. *La Pulga* raised his hands toward the sky, to pay tribute to his illustrious ancestor. Some time later, during an interview with the *TyC Sports* channel in Argentina, Leo revealed that the choice of the tribute had an unusual, overwhelming origin, typical of a story by Edgar Allan Poe: "I was lying the night before with Antonela [in the bedroom of their house in Barcelona, in the residential area of Bellamar, in Castelldefels]. It was around 11 at night, and I told her: 'I have to do something for Diego.' I have a museum upstairs with trophies and jerseys, and I went to see what there was, thinking about choosing a National Team shirt. I went up and, next to it, there is a little room where we keep things, with a little door that is always closed. But it was just open and, when I entered, I saw that on top of a chair: there was the Newell's No. 10 shirt [which Diego himself had used in 1993]. But that door is always closed, I don't know what I was doing there, really, because I didn't even remember I had it. It was incredible!" Messi took the jersey that appeared mysteriously and the next day he wore it to pay tribute to the eternal Maradona.

COPA AMÉRICA

In June 2021, Brazil once again hosted the Copa América. It should have been organized jointly by Argentina and Colombia in 2020, but it was postponed due to the coronavirus pandemic. After the pandemic, the tournament moved relocated to Brazil, with little explanation from CONMEBOL, the South American Football Confederation. Lionel Messi and his teammates didn't complain too much either: the change allowed them to take revenge in the same land where they had been wronged two years before.

All the matches were played without a crowd (albeit with a ridiculous ambient sound recording that tried uselessly to disguise the deserted stands), except for the final, which allowed about 5,000 fans to attend. In the Albiceleste squad's opening match against Chile, Leo opened the scoring with a masterful free kick that went into the right corner past goalkeeper Claudio Bravo, his former teammate at FC Barcelona. The match ended 1-1, and then Argentina beat Uruguay and Paraguay by the same score: 1-0. Next, the light blue and white team crushed Bolivia 4-1, with Messi scoring twice. *La Pulga* scored his fourth and last goal of the tournament against Ecuador in the quarterfinals. In the semifinal, a goalpost denied Leo what may have been the winning goal against Colombia. The duel ended 1-1 and Messi converted his penalty in the tiebreaker. The Argentine goalkeeper Emiliano *Dibu* Martínez became the hero of the day by saving three Colombian shots that catapulted his team to the final against Brazil, at the legendary Maracanã stadium in Rio de Janeiro.

NUMBERS

Players with the most titles in the Spanish League:

Player	Club	Titles
Francisco Gento	Real Madrid	12
Lionel Messi	FC Barcelona	10
José Pirri Martínez Sánchez	Real Madrid	10
Andrés Iniesta	FC Barcelona	9
Amanico Amora	Real Madrid	9
Carlos Santillana Alonso González	Real Madrid	9
José Antonio Camacho	Real Madrid	9

THE CARDS

In Rio de Janeiro, days before the 2021 Copa América final, Argentina stayed at the Windsor hotel in Barra da Tijuca. The tournament organizers had offered the Sheraton, but the players, led by captain Lionel Messi, rejected it: the national team had stayed there before the fateful 2014 World Cup final. The night before the big match against Brazil, Messi, Ángel di María, Leandro Paredes, Nicolás Otamendi, and Kun Sergio Agüero met in Rodrigo de Paul and Alejandro *Papu Gómez's* room to play cards with a Spanish deck. But, instead of the usual game (called *truco*), the hosts asked their companions to participate in a bizarre proposal: choose a card, which had to be in the first ten that were turned over from the deck of 40. If everyone got it right, they would take it as a positive prediction for the match against Brazil, and if the next day the national team actually became champion, everyone had to get a tattoo of their chosen card. In the documentary *Sean Eternos: Campeones de America*, Gómez said that he opted for the ace of clubs, which came out in 10th place. "Screams, hugs. Tomorrow we win!", the boys howled. Di María's six of clubs appeared first. "It seemed like a goal, it was crazy!" *Fideo* recalled. Otamendi's seven of swords emerged also almost immediately. More squealing, more screaming, more frenzy. Messi preferred the five of cups (like in a Spanish deck of cards). Why? Because he had already lost four finals (four cups) with the national team. The fifth time would be "the winner," he claimed. The card took a while: one, two, three . . . eight, nine . . . and it was the last card! "There, we can't lose," *Papu* mused in the midst of the general merriment.

ANOTHER RECORD

June 29, 2021: Lionel Messi broke the record for the number of games played by a soccer player with the Argentine national team. The match against Bolivia for the 2021 Copa América in Brazil put Leo at 148 games, surpassing Javier Mascherano by one, with whom, until that moment, he shared first place.

QUENCHING THE THIRST

After much frustration and four lost finals, Lionel Messi finally had the pleasure of lifting a trophy wearing the Argentine national team shirt. On July 10, 2021, at the Maracanã stadium in Rio de Janeiro, the Albiceleste squad defeated Brazil 0-1. In front of some 2,000 Argentine fans, who brought color and energy to the South American classic, Leo quenched the thirst for a lap of honor as vast as the Sahara Desert, as the match was decided with a single goal from Ángel *Fideo* di María. "The truth is that I needed to get rid of the thorn of being able to achieve something with the National Team. I had been close for many years, but I knew that at some point it was going to go wrong, it was going to happen. I am grateful to God for giving me this moment, in Brazil beating Brazil. He was saving that moment for me," the Argentine leader celebrated excitedly with his medal around his neck and the old silver trophy in his hands. Of course, Leo got the Spanish five of cups card tattooed on his left calf.

Messi finally managed to establish himself as the top scorer of a South American championship in his sixth Copa América. Leo began competing in the continental tournament in Peru 2007, and after participating in Argentina in 2011, Chile in 2015, US in 2016, and Brazil in 2019, only in Brazil 2021 did he secure his place as top scorer, with four goals. Of course, he shared that achievement with Colombian striker Luis Díaz, who also scored a total of four goals throughout the competition.

In the world of soccer, which is very difficult, there are many very false people."
(Lionel Messi, in a report published on September 5, 2020, by the Catalan newspaper *Mundo Deportivo*.)

DEPARTURE FROM BARCELONA

With the celebrations for the Copa América victory concluded, Lionel Messi returned to Barcelona . . . but not to FC Barcelona. On Thursday, August 5, 2021, the Catalan club—chaired since March of that year by Joan Laporta—issued a statement that paralyzed the soccer world that despite FC Barcelona and Lionel Messi had reached an agreement and the clear intention of both parties to sign a new contract, this couldn't happen because of Spanish LaLiga regulations on player registration. As a result, Messi was not going to be staying on at FC Barcelona. Both parties deeply regretted that the wishes of the player and the club were not ultimately fulfilled. FC Barcelona wholeheartedly expressed its gratitude to the player for his contribution to the aggrandizement of the club and wished him all the very best for his future.

The next day, Laporta gave a press conference in which he assured that "there was no margin to keep Messi," and blamed previous managements for having left "a disastrous inheritance" with "a salary mass outside the limit" of the economic possibilities of the club. The manager highlighted that Leo "has behaved excellently and the proof is that he wanted to stay. The player has done his best to make things easy." However, Laporta explained that he had to give up retaining the greatest star in *culé* history because he was not willing to "mortgage" the club's economy "for half a century," and stated that "above players, coaches, presidents, of managers, there is the entity: FC Barcelona. An institution with more than 120 years of history."

ACHIEVEMENTS

Lionel Messi played 778 games with the FC Barcelona first team, scoring 672 goals (an average of 0.86 goals per game) and providing 269 assists. *La Pulga* won 34 official titles, including 10 Spanish leagues and four UEFA Champions Leagues.

GOODBYE

Two days after Joan Laporta's announcements, Lionel Messi appeared before the media from around the world at the Auditori 1899, located a few meters from FC Barcelona's Camp Nou. Very sad and at times overcome by tears, Leo, accompanied by his wife Antonela and his three children, acknowledged that leaving the *Barça* club fell on him "like a bucket of cold water. I was not prepared. This is very difficult for me, after so many years of living my entire life here. We were convinced, my family and I, that we were going to continue here, in our house, which was what we wanted most: to continue enjoying this life we have in Barcelona, both in sports as well as in everyday life, which is wonderful." Messi revealed that he had offered to halve his salary to continue at the club, but it was not enough to enable him to stay. "I arrived when I was very young, 13 years old. After 21 years, I'm leaving with my wife, with three Argentinian Catalans. I couldn't be more proud of everything I did," he continued. Excited, Lionel highlighted that "I would have liked to say goodbye in a different way, with people on the field, to be able to hear one last ovation from them, one last love," and he remarked: "I hope I can return to this club, in whatever way. I hope can contribute something so that this club continues to be the best in the world."

DROP IN FINANCES

Once Lionel Messi's departure was common knowledge, the consultancy firm Brand Finance estimated that the departure of the Argentine star would equate to an annual loss of €137 million for FC Barcelona, as a result in a drop in the sale of shirts and tickets to matches, a decrease in advertising agreements, the value of the team for friendly games, and reduced prize money in the event of poorer sporting results. Indeed, in the 2021/22 season, FC Barcelona did not win any titles and was eliminated from the UEFA Champions League in the group stage, something that had never happened during the Messi Era. According to the consulting firm, sales of shirts with the number "10" on the back alone had generated more than €200 million in 2020, of which about €30 million remained for the club.

PARIS

August 10, 2021: Lionel Messi arrived with his family in the capital of France, dressed in a white sports T-shirt with a black letter print on the chest: Ici c'est Paris (Here is Paris). Then, at the Parc des Princes stadium, he signed a two-year agreement with the PSG club, and posed with an official shirt bearing the number 30—the same number he wore at the start of his career with FC Barcelona.

REUNITED WITH TEAMMATES

"I love soccer, I enjoy it like a child and I want to continue winning titles, and PSG was the best place to do it." Measured, quickly recovered from the disappointing end at FC Barcelona, Lionel Messi appeared in the auditorium of the Parc des Princes to officially introduce himself as the new player of the Parisian team. Wearing a dark blue suit, a white cotton shirt, and a silk tie with blue and black patterns, La Pulga assured: "Now, my happiness is enormous," and stressed that one of the reasons for his choice of new team was the possibility of playing alongside two of his teammates in the Argentine national team, Ángel di María and Leandro Paredes, as well as reuniting with the Brazilian Neymar, with whom he had cultivated an intense friendship during his time at Barça. "Playing with Neymar and (the Frenchman Kylian) Mbappé is crazy. Spectacular signings have been made. I am very excited to start training and competing. I will do it with the best and that is always nice and beautiful," he explained.

There are three or four important things in life: Books, friends and women . . . and Messi."

(Portuguese writer António Lobo Antunes, in an interview given to the Spanish newspaper *El País*, in January 2012.)

PARISIAN DEBUT

Lionel Messi joined PSG three days after the 2021/22 season began, but didn't make his debut until August 29, when he replaced his Brazilian friend Neymar in the 66th minute of the match against the Stade de Reims at the Auguste-Delaune stadium. The Parisian squad won 0-2, and Leo took the pitch when the score was already decided. *La Pulga* started for the first time on September 19 against Olympique Lyonnaise, at the Parc des Princes. The first goal? It did not arrive in Ligue 1, but in the UEFA Champions League, against Pep Guardiola's Manchester City, whom he once again defeated. The Argentine star scored the second goal of a 2-0 victory in Paris. In Ligue 1, the first hit on the net came against FC Nantes on match day 14.

Although they lost four games, the blue and red team won the local league very comfortably, finishing 15 points ahead of second-placed Olympique de Marseille. *La Pulga* appeared in 26 games, only scoring six goals (his lowest record since the 2005/06 season at FC Barcelona) and 14 assists.

The first setback of the season was on January 31, 2022, in the French Cup, where PSG fell in the round of 16 against OG Nice, on penalties. Leo—who had missed several games due to having contracted Covid-19 during the Christmas and New Year celebrations in Rosario—converting a penalty kick, but Paredes and Xavier Simons missed, and PSG was eliminated.

NEAPOLITAN MILANESE

Lionel Messi's favorite food is Neapolitan Milanese: a fine beef steak breaded and fried, then baked with a layer of tomato sauce and melted mozzarella-type cheese on top. Leo requested this delicacy in several famous restaurants in Europe and Argentina, but he declared that the best Neapolitan Milanese in the world is prepared by his mother, Celia. "Others tried it and ended up saying that it's true, that their milanesas are the best. Maybe it's the sauce they have on top," *La Pulga* mused.

SPONSORSHIP

In April 2002, Lionel Messi, then 14 years old, signed a sponsorship deal to wear Nike soccer shoes. When the contract ended, the American company offered to renew the contract for €180,000 per year. However, according to the news portal *Márketing Deportivo*, the German giant adidas made an irresistible counteroffer: €600,000 per year. Leo accepted, and from March 2006 he began to wear the iconic three stripes, signing a lifetime deal with adidas. *La Pulga* wears soccer shoes in size 42 (8.5 according to the American size system).

NUMBERS

Top scorers with the Argentine national team (until December 2024):

Player	Goals	Games
Lionel Messi	112	189
Gabriel Batistuta	54	77
Sergio Agüero	41	101
Hernán Crespo	35	64
Diego Maradona	34	91

PROGRESS HALTED

Also in the round of 16, Paris's progress in the 2021/22 UEFA Champions League was cut short by Real Madrid: PSG won the first leg 1-0 at the Parc des Princes. On March 9, at the Santiago Bernabéu stadium, the French side extended their lead with a goal from Kylian Mbappé, and it seemed that their qualification was on track. However, with half an hour to go, PSG's Italian goalkeeper, Gianluigi Donnarumma, made a costly error by trying to come out playing with his feet, instead of sending the ball out of the pitch, handing possession to his rivals, and Frenchman

Karim Benzema equalized. Two more goals from Benzema gave Real Madrid put an end to PSG's dreams.

SEVENTH BALLON D'OR

November 29, 2021: Lionel Messi received his seventh Ballon d'Or, beating the Polish striker of Bayern München, Robert Lewandowski, and the Brazilian Jorge *Jorginho* Luiz Frello Filho of the English club Chelsea, who had won the Champions League 2020/21. Leo won the trophy for having won his first Copa América, his seventh Copa del Rey with FC Barcelona, and having reached his eighth Pichichi Trophy before leaving the Catalan team.

UNDEFEATED

Argentina qualified undefeated for the 2022 World Cup in Qatar, with Lionel Messi playing a key role. He was the team's top scorer in that preliminary competition, along with Lautaro Martínez, with seven goals each. Leo played in 15 games, only missing two duels at the start of 2022 because he had not fully recovered from Covid-19. Since the round robin format was introduced for the ten countries participating in the South American Qualifiers for the 1998 French World Cup, Argentina had never made it through the qualifiers undefeated. The last time the Albiceleste team had qualified for the World Cup without losing was in the qualification for West Germany 1974, although on that occasion Argentina only faced Bolivia and Paraguay in a short triangular series.

You can only stop Messi with a machine gun."
(Hilarious occurrence expressed by former FC Barcelona player Hristo Stoichkov to the Bulgarian newspaper *Trud*, in April 2010.)

DEFEAT

Lionel Messi, his teammates, and the coaching staff of the Albiceleste team arrived at the Qatar University grounds, which would be their home during the 2022 World Cup, with the latent dream of the third star on the shield of the AFA. Leo, like no one else, dreamed with all his might of being champion, of lifting the only trophy that, until then, had been denied to him.

For the first time, the most important soccer tournament did not take place between the months of June and July. The selection of Qatar as host forced FIFA to modify the schedule because temperatures in those months are usually around 37 degrees on a daily average. The competition was moved to November and December, the "winter" time of the Middle Eastern country, when temperatures range between 20 and 25 degrees. The Argentine national team appeared in Qatar undefeated in 36 games in South American tournaments, the Qualifiers, and friendlies. In the group stage, they were drawn against three rivals who, before the start of the Cup, seemed to be easy prey for the Copa América champions: Saudi Arabia, Mexico, and Poland. However, World Cups have always been characterized by surprises, and the Qatari championship was no exception. On November 22, at the Lusail Stadium, Argentina came out aggressively against its Saudi rival, taking the lead after 10 minutes, with a penalty converted by Leo. The South American side continued to bombard the rival goal, to the point of reaching the Saudi net three more times in the first half, but all the conquests were disallowed for offside. It seemed that an Argentine rout was inevitable in the second stage, but the Arab squad turned the score around in just eight minutes, with two goals from Saleh Al-Shehri and Salem Al-Dawsari. The score did not change and the Albiceleste team lost for the first time in a World Cup against an Asian rival. "We know that it is a defeat that hurts, but we have to continue trusting in ourselves. Let the people trust, that this group is not going to leave them stranded and we are going to try to beat Mexico to settle back in," *La Pulga* declared to the journalists after the match. Leo took the blow, but had not been knocked out. His hopes remained intact: he knew there were still chances to lift the Cup, but no margin for error. He just had to trust in his magic. Throughout his professional career, he had pulled many rabbits out of his hat.

TRIBUTE TO MARADONA

On November 25, 2022, two years after the death of Diego Maradona, Lionel Messi made a post on his Instagram social network account to remember the great Albiceleste star who won the Mexican World Cup in 1986. "It is strange not to see him in the stands, not to see people go crazy when he appears, what he transmitted, what he made the rest feel. It will be special if he is not present. He loved the National Team. He was always there and always will be with us from somewhere," Leo said in his message.

HARD-EARNED VICTORY

Four days after the defeat against Saudi Arabia, the Argentine team returned to the grass of the Lusail Stadium to face Mexico—a rival that was seeking revenge after being eliminated by the Albiceleste squad in the round of 16 in the 2006 and 2010 World Cups. A draw seemed like a good result for the Aztec squad. The South American team, which needed all three points no matter what, came out to devour its opponent, but didn't manage to find a way past Francisco Guillermo Ochoa in goal. After a modest and goalless first half, in the 64th minute, the great Leo produced a masterpiece: he received the ball outside the Mexican penalty area and fired a devastating left-footed shot that sank into the net just inside the goalkeeper's left post. The Albiceleste advantage became unattainable for the Aztecs in the 87th minute, when Enzo Fernández sent the ball into Ochoa's top left corner.

With three points in hand, Argentina appeared in violet shirts to compete for first place in the group against Poland, on November 30 at Stadium 974—named because it was built on a base of 974 recycled containers and for sharing the international telephone dialing code for Qatar, Doha. *La Pulga* and his teammates advanced repeatedly to their rival's goal, which turned goalkeeper Wojciech Szczęsny into a star—the same player who had admired FC Barcelona's soccer style when his team, AS Rome, lost 6-1. At 36 minutes, Dutch referee Danny Makkelie awarded a penalty to the South Americans for an alleged foul by Szczęsny on Messi. Leo took the shot, but the keeper saved it. The Albiceleste captain's mistake did not dampen the team's spirit. On the contrary, Argentina continued to attack fiercely. In the first minute of the second half, Nahuel Molina broke through the Polish defense and with a cut pass connected by Alexis Mac Allister. The shot lacked power, but was still unreachable for Szczęsny. Twenty minutes later, Julián Alvarez received a cut pass from Enzo Fernández and sent the ball into the net of the European goal—a great goal that secured qualification for the second phase and relieved so much pent-up anguish.

ALBICELESTE VICTORY

In the round of 16 of the World Cup in Qatar, Australia crossed the path of the light blue and white team. In the 35th, a magical touch from Lionel Messi's left foot sailed through a tangle of legs and hit Mathew Ryan's right goalpost. At 57, Julián Alvarez took advantage of a mistake by Ryan to send the ball into the net. With the margin on the scoreboard widened, the situation seemed under control *La Pulga's* squad. However, in the 77th minute Australia scored, and at the last second, the Albiceleste goalkeeper Emiliano Martínez deactivated a powerful shot by forward Garang Kuol, who had been left alone in front of the goal. "I'm happy for this victory and for taking another step. We have to stay united," Leo said.

In the next phase, back to Lusail to face the Netherlands, Lionel Messi had a starring role: at 35 minutes into the first half, *La Pulga*, surrounded by six players in orange, gave a pinpoint pass to Nahuel Molina who, with a well-placed kick, broke the deadlock against goalkeeper Andries Noppert. In the 73rd minute, Leo converted a new penalty, after a foul on Marcos Acuña. After the goal, Messi approached the Dutch bench, led by Louis van Gaal, raised his hands to his head and placed them behind his ears, to listen to the reactions of the European coaching staff. Fifteen minutes from the end, Argentina flourished. But the orange-clad coach sent a giant almost 2 meters tall, Wout Weghorst, onto the field and the score began to even out. First, the lean 1.97-meter striker scored in the 82nd with a header. Then, the Spanish referee Mateu Lahoz awarded a free kick to the Netherlands in the 101st minute—the judge had awarded 12 minutes of extra time. While the Argentine defense was waiting for another cross to the roof of the orange giants, the left-footed Teun Koopmeiners played low toward Weghorst who, despite the efforts of Enzo Fernández, managed to equalize. After some very dramatic extra time—throughout the match, the judge showed 16 yellow cards and one red, setting a World Cup record—in which Argentina had increasing opportunities to decide the match, it eventually had to be decided by penalties. Emiliano Martínez, once again the hero, saved the first two European penalties from Van Dijk and Steven Berghuis. The successful conversions of Messi, Paredes, Montiel, and Lautaro Martínez secured the Albiceleste victory. "We suffer too much unfairly. Van Gaal sells that he plays soccer well and puts tall people in so they can throw balls at him," Messi said when interviewed by *TyC Sports* after the match.

1,000 GAMES

December 3, 2022: By playing against Australia in the 2022 World Cup in Qatar, Lionel Messi reached 1,000 official matches, including appearances with the first team of FC Barcelona (778), PSG (53), and the Argentina national team (169). "I don't think about that. I found out today, I thought there was more to go. I live in the moment and enjoy the moment of what we are going through," said the Argentine star after the match, when asked by the press. In those 1,000 games, Leo totaled 789 goals and 348 assists.

OUTBURSTS

After the victory over the Netherlands, Lionel Messi coined a phrase that would become a meme, merchandising, t-shirts and mugs, history. While Leo was being interviewed by a journalist from the *TyC Sports* channel, the Dutch giant Wout Weghorst approached him with a very bitter expression. Messi, very angry, avoided him. The Orange scorer put his arms on his hips and fixed his grim gaze on *La Pulga*, who, without noticing that he was appearing live on television, launched a phrase that would go around the world on social networks: "What are you looking at, bobo? What are you looking at, bobo? Go over there, bobo, go over there." Some time later, during an interview with *Urbana Play* radio, Messi acknowledged having two outbursts in front of van Gaal—when he grabbed his ears after his goal, as a sign of mockery—and in front of Weghorst: "I don't like what I did, or what I said afterwards. They are moments of great tension, of great nervousness, and everything happens very quickly: you don't have time to think about anything and you react the way you react. I don't like leaving that image behind."

Boys, Now we've got our hopes up again, I want to win the third, I want to be world champion."

(The song by the group *La Mosca* that became an anthem in Argentina, and in many countries where Lionel Messi is an idol, during the 2022 World Cup in Qatar.)

EPIC

Epic is how the performance of Lionel Messi and the Argentine team against Croatia in the semifinal of the Qatar 2022 World Cup should be rated—once again at the Lusail Stadium. *La Pulga's* performance was amazing: with a penalty goal, after a foul by goalkeeper Dominik Livaković against Julián Alvarez, he opened the scoring in the 34th minute. Later, with the match in the South American squad's favor 2-0, Leo delivered a wonderful performance, including a tremendous dribble past the award-winning center back Joško Gvardiol, which Alvarez sent into the net for the 3-0 score. "We are going to play the last game, which is what we wanted," celebrated the Albiceleste captain at the end of the semifinal. "I'm really enjoying this, beyond the fact that we started by losing. We ask people to trust, we know what we are: this group is crazy. Once again Argentina is in a world final, let's enjoy all this. We knew that we could do it, we have a lot of confidence. Everything we did was on our own merit, game by game," he added.

PENALTIES

Lionel Messi took the most penalty kicks in a single edition of the World Cup. In Qatar 2022, *La Pulga* shot five times from the spot marked with lime: once against Saudi Arabia, once against Poland (the goalkeeper saved Wojciech Szczęsny), another against the Netherlands, the fourth against Croatia, and the fifth in the final with France. The two penalties from the shootout against the orange and blue teams are not included in that tally. Until then, the records for the most penalties taken in a single World Cup edition belonged to the Portuguese Eusébio, who took four in the 1966 England tournament, and the Dutch Rob Rensenbrink, who also took four in the 1978 World Cup. Eusébio and Rensenbrink scored on all of their attempts.

THIRD GOLD STAR

The Qatar World Cup final, starring Argentina and France on December 18, 2022, at the Lusail Stadium, is without a doubt, the most exciting in the history of the tournament. Never has a World Cup definition been so exciting, electrifying, moving. Led by a brilliant Lionel Messi, the Albiceleste team took a 2-0 lead, with a goal from *La Pulga*, from a penalty, and another from Ángel di María, after an extraordinary collective move. Argentina, who maintained control of the ball in the second half, generated more scoring opportunities but, similarly to the match against the Netherlands, lost the advantage. France equalized with a double from Kylian Mbappé: first from a penalty, a few seconds later with an unstoppable volley. The 90 minutes ended 2-2 and, in extra time, Leo, joining the South American attack, took advantage of a rebound off French goalkeeper Hugo Lloris to score his team's third goal . . . with his right foot! Just 90 seconds later, Polish referee Szymon Marciniak awarded another penalty for France, which Mbappé converted into the final tie. Messi was on the verge of being left empty-handed in the last moments of the match, when the Frenchman Kolo Muani found himself alone with the ball in front of Emiliano Martínez, but the left foot of the phenomenal goalkeeper saved the goal.

The most astonishing and dramatic final of the soccer World Cup was decided from the penalty spot. Messi, Paulo Dybala, and Leandro Paredes, infallible, scored their goals; Dibu Martínez, outstanding, saved Kingsley Coman's shot with his chest, unsettling Aurélien Tchouaméni to miss wide of the goal. With Argentina leading 3-2, Gonzalo Montiel destroyed 36 years of anguish for the Argentine fans, fulfilling a lifelong dream for Lionel Messi to lift the most coveted trophy in soccer, and in all of sport.

"Look what it is! It's beautiful. Do you know how much I'm going to kiss it? I wanted it so much! We suffered a lot, but we got it," Leo was excited before the *TyC Sports* cameras, hugging the gold-plated trophy, and wrapped in a black, gold-trimmed cloak—*bisht*—a gift from the hosts. The Rosario star had just fulfilled his greatest personal wish, and also that of the Argentine fans: that the light blue and white shirt would receive its third gold star.

NUMBERS

Players with the most games as captain in the World Cup:

Player	Games	Captain
Lionel Messi (Argentina)	26	19
Diego Maradona (Argentina)	21	16
Rafael Márquez (Mexico)	19	15*
Cristiano Ronaldo (Portugal)	21	14
Dino Zoff (Italy)	17	14

**In Mexico Márquez is credited with 17, but in two of those games he did not enter as captain: he received the armband from Andrés Guardado when he left the field.*

RECORDS BROKEN

At the 2022 World Cup in Qatar, Lionel Messi broke several records. It has been highlighted that Leo is one of the players with the most World Cups played (5), the most games played (26), and with the most appearances as captain of his team (19). But he is also the oldest player to score a goal in a final (he was 35 years and 177 days old when he scored against France in Doha, on December 18, 2022), and the first to score a goal in the group stage, round of 16 final, quarterfinals, semifinal, and final of the same tournament. He also established himself as the player with the most minutes on the field: 2,314. *La Pulga* surpassed the Italian Paolo Maldini, with 2,220 minutes.

CROWD ADORATION

December 20, 2022: The world champions, led by Lionel Messi, returned to Buenos Aires, the Argentine capital, intending to celebrate the conquest of the World Cup in Qatar on an open-top bus. But an adoring crowd estimated at 5 million people flooded the roads, preventing the vehicle's progress. The players left the bus and boarded police helicopters to enjoy, from the air, the exciting display of adoration.

TRIBUTE IN THE FIELDS

To celebrate winning the World Cup in the Qatar 2022 tournament, one Argentine agronomist planted a field with different types of seeds and different densities, which, when grown and observed from the sky, was a reproduction of the face of . . . Lionel Messi! This curious work of art, made in the province of San Luis, cost US$459. "Giving a smile to those who fly overhead is priceless," said engineer Nicolás Ríos Centeno. The most notable thing is that several agricultural producers asked him to repeat the experience in their fields. "It's a farmer's fun, it's the desire to have a good time at work and doing things," declared Ríos Centeno. But he was not the only one who celebrated the Cup with an agricultural undertaking: engineer Carlos Faricelli also designed an image of the Argentine captain in his corn plantation in the province of Córdoba. Similarly to Ríos Centeno, several farmers asked him to copy the plantation on their properties.

I would like to be remembered as someone who tried. That is my message to the new generation that loves me and defends me so much."

(Emotional confession by Lionel Messi during a report on the *Olga* streaming channel, in August 2023.)

AU REVOIR

Lionel Messi's second season at PSG was disappointing for *Rouge et Bleu* fans. Although the team won the Ligue 1, it did so by just one point ahead of the runner-up, Racing Club de Lens, and with seven defeats under its belt, four of them at the Parc des Princes. Individually, Leo had a good campaign: he participated in 32 games, scored 21 goals, and provided 16 assists. But what upset Parisian fans the most was the quick elimination in the European Champions League, against Bayern München, in the round of 16. The fans were not happy with a team with the greatest players of the Qatar World Cup—champion Messi, and the runner-up and top scorer Kylian Mbappé, scorer of eight goals, as well as other stars such as the Brazilian Neymar—but fell against the German team, 0-1 in Paris and 2-0 in Munich. Hours before the last match of the League against Clermont Foot in the French capital, PSG coach Christophe Galtier anticipated *La Pulga's* departure: "I had the enormous privilege of coaching the best player in history. Saturday is his last game at the Parc des Princes," he announced during a press conference. A few hours later, the club, quickly, uploaded a video to its social networks with the best actions of its number 30 and a farewell phrase: "PSG would like to warmly thank the seven-time Ballon d'Or champion, winner under the blue and red colors of a Super Cup and two French national championships." After the match against Clermont, Leo confirmed his departure: "I am happy to have represented PSG and I have really enjoyed playing with this team and with these great players. I want to thank the club for this wonderful experience in Paris," he responded to a journalist from the *ESPN* network.

THE GOLDEN FOOT

On several occasions, sports writers have compared Lionel Messi's left foot to gold. This metaphor became a reality in March 2013, when a Japanese jewelry store called Ginza Tanaka took a mold of Leo's left limb and made a sculpture called The Golden Foot. The jewel, produced with 25 kilos of gold, was sold in at auction for €5 million. The money was donated by Messi and Ginza Tanaka to a foundation dedicated to assisting children in vulnerable situations.

MIAMI

"I'm going to Miami," Lionel Messi reported on June 7, 2023, during an interview that he gave jointly to two Catalan newspapers: Sport and Mundo Deportivo. "I was eager, very excited to be able to return (to FC Barcelona) but on the other hand, after having experienced what I experienced, the exit I had, I did not want to go through that situation or leave my future in the hands of another. I wanted to make my own decision, thinking about me and my family," stated La Pulga. Furthermore, he indicated that, for his return to be consolidated, the Barça club "had to sell players or lower salaries, and the truth is that I did not want to go through that." In that report, Leo acknowledged that during his stay in Paris "I was not happy, I did not enjoy it, and that affected my family life. They were two difficult years that are now behind me. I missed many things about my children." He stressed that the choice of Inter Miami CF was based on "returning, in quotes, to reconnect with my family, with my children, to enjoy everyday life. I was lucky to have achieved everything in soccer and today I look beyond what sports, which interests me a lot, but more about family and my well-being," "If it had been a question of money," he stressed, "I would have gone to Arabia or somewhere else where they offered me a lot of money, but the truth is that my decision lies elsewhere." A few hours later, the Florida state club officially confirmed the hiring of the Argentine star, triggering a true sporting revolution throughout the US. Just one hour after the official announcement was made, the pink club had doubled its number of followers on Instagram, along with the demand for individual tickets for the rest of the championship and season tickets for the next. Messi-mania spread beyond Florida: for the match between LA Galaxy and Inter Miami at the MLS 2024 at the Dignity Health Sports Park, tickets were sold out in—in under six minutes!

ALFAJORES

In 2013, Carlos Marconi, who had worked as coordinator of the children's soccer school of the Newell's Old Boys club in the city of Rosario when Lionel Messi played there, revealed in an interview with *TN Deportivo* that he used to reward his young players with sweets that he bought at the kiosk of the red and black sports complex. On one occasion, after noticing that Leo was a fan of triple *alfajores* (sandwich cookie), Marconi made a proposal to *La Pulga*:

For every goal you score, I give you an alfajor.

The manager realized very soon that his offer would leave him bankrupt: Leo scored four or five goals per game. To try to save his finances, Marconi substantially modified his initiative:

Let's do another thing: from now on, I'm going to give you two alfajores . . . but for every goal you score with your head.

Lionel, mischievous, accepted the challenge with a smile: in the next match, he eluded all his rivals, including the goalkeeper, and centimeters from the goal line he lifted the ball and headed it to the net. Then, he ran toward the stand where Marconi was and showed him his hand closed with two fingers in a "v" to announce that he owed him two alfajores. In that match, Messi scored three times with headers, so the reward cost the brave coach dearly.

After the match, Marconi and Leo met at the kiosk: the young player received the six *alfajores* and distributed them among his six teammates. Moved, Marconi bought an extra cookie, gave it to *La Pulga* and told him:

You didn't earn this alfajor for being a good player, nor for having scored a goal: I give it to you for being a good person.

INTER MIAMI

July 16, 2023: Lionel Messi was officially presented as a new Inter Miami player at the Drive Pink Stadium in the city of Fort Lauderdale, located north of Miami-Dade County. "I want to thank all of Miami for this welcome, this affection. The truth is that I am very excited to be here with you," Leo said during the ceremony, presided over by the club's owners: businessmen Jorge and José Mas and the Former English player David Beckham. "I am very happy to have chosen this city with my family, this project. I have no doubt that we are going to have a great time," says *La Pulga*.

SUCCESS

Lionel Messi's campaign at Inter Miami started successfully. Leo made his debut with the pink shirt during the Leagues Cup, a tournament featuring teams from the US and Mexico. On July 21, a goal from *La Pulga* secured victory to The Herons at home against Cruz Azul, 2-1, in the group stage. Four days later, a double by Leo opened a 4-0 beating of Atlanta United, again in Fort Lauderdale. Messi repeated the pair of goals in the knockout stage of the competition: first, in the 3-1 victory against Orlando City SC, then in a 4-4 draw against Dallas FC at Toyota Stadium. In this match, Lionel also converted his penalty in the shootout that decided the game in favor of the Florida team, 3-5. In the quarterfinals, a new victory by *La Pulga* rounded off a huge 4-0 victory over Charlotte FC, at the Drive Pink Stadium. At Subaru Park in Chester, Pennsylvania, Messi once again got his name on the scoreboard in another win: 1-4 against Philadelphia Union in the semi. The final took place on August 19 at Geodis Park, home of Nashville SC. Leo, naturally, scored his team's only goal for the final 1-1, and also converted his attempt in the penalty shootout that decided the tournament in favor of the Miami team, with a 9-10 win! This tiebreaker was especially remarkable because all 11 players from each team took a shot, and it was decided by a double victory by goalkeeper Drake Callender, who scored with his right foot and saved the final attempt from Elliot Panicco. Just one month after arriving in Miami, Lionel Messi secured his first title in his pink shirt. Furthermore, he not only established himself as the top scorer of the championship but he scored in every game. An extraordinary performance worthy of his award-winning resume.

Get up, try again and again. That's the message for the kids who follow me, who like to see me, not only for soccer but for life, because that's life: stumble, get up and fight for your dreams". (Lionel Messi motivating his fans, during an interview for Fox Sport Radio in May 2019)

ADORATION

In this book, many crazy anecdotes of Lionel Messi in stadiums around the world have already been reported. But there are many more left! Before the Albiceleste team faced Curaçao in a friendly held in the Argentine city of Santiago del Estero, on March 28, 2023, the captain of the Caribbean squad, Cuco Martina, asked Leo to give him 23 shirts with the 10 and the surname of the Rosario star printed on the back! The unusual request was made hours before in the hotel where the Curaçao soccer players were staying, when everyone had an unexpected discussion about who would be chosen to exchange their jersey with *La Pulga*. "We are 23 players. Please arrange 23 shirts for us," Martina implored. But the South American kit manager, the one who kept the star's jersey, was goalkeeper Eloy Room, didn't have enough stock to meet demand. Speaking on television in the Netherlands, the Columbus Crew goalkeeper, of the US MLS, explained that he had asked his Argentine teammate Lucas Zelarrayán for help: "At the end of the first half," he said, "it occurred to me to walk next to him towards the locker room tunnel. I asked Messi about his shirt and he immediately told me that it was fine, that he would give it to me after the game. I kept thinking: maybe he says that now, but later he will forget. When the referee gave the whistle, Messi was close to the area, but he was moving away from me. I called him. He immediately reacted as if he were saying 'oh yes, the shirts'. So I approached him. and he gave it to me. Right away, he asked for mine, so we exchanged them." Room returned to the locker room happy: his prize dispelled the bitterness of suffering seven goals from the world champions. Of those seven goals, three were at the hand of the person who had just given him his shirt.

A few months later, shortly before Argentina faced Australia in a friendly scheduled for June 15, 2023, at the Workers' Stadium in Beijing, China, *La Pulga* received a request for an autograph from . . . one of the linesmen! The assistant, named Zhou Fei, approached Leo before the teams went out onto the playing field. He had a notebook and a pen that he had in his pocket and, without blushing, asked the Argentine Ten to sign a sheet of paper. A little while later, a ball boy repeated the request for an autograph and, while the game was going on, a local fan entered the field wearing an Albiceleste shirt, approached his idol and hugged him. The police then detained the intruder and took him into custody. Apparently, the boy cared little about the punishment: his dream had come true. Furthermore, the excitement to see Leo was demonstrated by the sale of tickets for that friendly match: the 68,000 tickets—with values ranging between US$82 and US$675—were sold out just a few minutes after going on sale. The 40,000 tickets for a friendly that Inter Miami played in Hong Kong against a local team were also sold out in less than an hour. Notably, the 40,000 seats at the Hong Kong Stadium were also sold out to watch a training session of the visiting soccer players the day before the match.

Another incident that demonstrates the devotion to *La Pulga* happened when Argentina visited Peru for the 2026 World Cup Qualifiers, in October 2023: many of the local fans who arrived at the National

Stadium in Lima wore their team's traditional white shirt with a red band crossed diagonally, with the number 10 and the name "Messi" engraved on the back. The Albiceleste team won 0-2 and Leo did not disappoint his Peruvian fans: he scored both goals.

LEONEL

"Lionel" was not going to be called that, but "Leonel." Or, at least, that was his mother's wish. When registering the birth of his third child, Jorge, perhaps confused, registered the baby as "Lionel," convinced that his wife, a fan of the American singer Lionel Richie, had mentioned that to him, and not "Leonel."

EIGHTH BALLON D'OR

The conquest of the 2022 World Cup in Qatar provided Lionel Messi with his eighth Ballon d'Or on a silver platter. The awards gala took place on October 30, 2023, and the directors of *France Football* magazine announced that Leo had won the vote over the Norwegian Erling Haaland—who a few months earlier had won the European Champions League with the English club Manchester City—and the Frenchman Kylian Mbappé, runner-up and top scorer in the Qatari tournament. "I want to share it with my teammates on the Argentine team. This is a gift for the entire group and for all the people of Argentina after what we achieved," *La Pulga* announced after receiving his trophy. "I got my dream, the last one I was lacking," he celebrated. Furthermore, he remembered his compatriot Diego Maradona, who died three years earlier, who would have turned 63 that same day: "I think there is no better place than here to wish him a happy birthday: surrounded by players, coaches, people who like soccer. Wherever you are, happy birthday, Diego. This is also for you, I share it with you and all of Argentina!"

NUMBERS

Top scorers in the World Cup (until Qatar 2022):

1	Miroslave Klose (Germany)	16
2	Ronaldo Nazário (Brazil)	15
3	Gerd Müller (Germany)	14
4	Just Fontaine (France)	13
5	Lionel Messi (Argentina)	13

TATTOOS

Lionel Messi's body is adorned with a countless collection of tattoos. Most of these illustrations are the work of artist Roberto López, well known in the Argentine soccer scene. López, who has traveled especially to Barcelona and Paris to attend to his most famous client, has created images such as ornaments from the Sagrada Família—the monumental unfinished basilica of the Catalan architect Antonio Gaudí—the face of Christ, a lotus flower, a portrait of Leo's mother, the hands of his first-born, Thiago, and the names of his other two children: Mateo and Ciro. He also tattooed the date of their marriage in Roman numerals on the ring fingers of Lionel and his wife, Antonela Roccuzzo, and are hidden under their wedding rings.

HERO WORSHIP

August 15, 2023: Inter Miami beat Philadelphia Union 1-4 in the Leagues Cup semifinal. After the match, the local "10", the Hungarian Dániel Gazdag approached Lionel Messi to greet him. "It's not the result we wanted, but I finally met my hero," Gazdag posted on his social media, along with a photo of him greeting *La Pulga*. Gréta Gáal, the Magyar player's girlfriend, responded to the post with an unusual reproach: "He never looked at me the way he looks at Messi."

MESSI'S FATHER

Lionel Messi's popularity has extended further than the football pitch. After the 2022 World Cup in Qatar, for example, "Lionel" became the most popular male name among new Argentine parents. This could be expected in a country where soccer has acquired religious status. But what happened in November 2017 in the city of General Roca, in the province of Río Negro was unexpected: a man showed up at the civil registry office to ask that his baby be registered with the name . . . Messi! Surprised, the authorities responded that this name was not approved and suggested to the new father that, like thousands of others, he choose "Lionel." The applicant remained firm and justified his preference by pointing out that "my wife and I really like 'Messi'. We admire him for the kind of person he is and for his humility." Given the man's persistence, civil registry officials agreed to consider the request. Ten (it couldn't be any other way) days later, the unusual name was authorized and the baby was registered as "Messi Daniel Varela." As soon as he received the birth certificate, the man proudly announced: "I am Messi's father."

Playing ball was always the fundamental thing, until the arrival of my first child. That automatically changes everything and there are other priorities before soccer."
(Lionel Messi expressed his feelings on the importance of family in a documentary *Messi Meets America* broadcast in December 2023 on Apple TV.)

AUCTIONS

In April 2022, a picture of Lionel Messi was auctioned for . . . US$522,000! The illustration, corresponding to a limited edition of trading cards called

Panini Prizm World Cup, produced by the Panini company, included a photograph of Leo with the Argentine jersey used in the 2014 World Cup in Brazil.

A few months later, in December 2023, six shirts used by *La Pulga* in the 2022 World Cup in Qatar were auctioned off for US$7.8 million. The sale was organized by the renowned Sotheby's house in New York. The lot included the Albiceleste jersey worn by Leo in the early stages of matches played against Saudi Arabia, Mexico, Australia, the Netherlands, Croatia, and France. The collection did not include any shirts used against Poland: in that match, Argentina wore its violet alternative kit. Part of the money raised in the auction was donated to the Sant Joan de Déu Children's Hospital in Barcelona for children suffering from rare diseases.

But, by far, the most incredible auction related to Leo happened in Argentina: in September 2023, the authorities of the Argentinos Juniors club decided to auction off the goals of their field, which needed to be renovated, through an app created for fans. One of the lots was presented as "the goal in which Nicolás González scored the promotion goal" to the First Division: on July 8, 2017, Argentinos defeated Gimnasia de Jujuy 1-0, with that goal from González marking their return to the First Division. One of the supporters, Christian Gutiérrez Alup, participated in the bidding and won the prize for only 185,000 *pesos*, approximately US$185 at that time. When Christian received the goal and the certificate of authenticity with the date of installation and removal from the field, he discovered that it had been the site of another historic goal . . . or, at least, one more historic than González's: Lionel Messi's first goal with the Argentine national team shirt, scored on June 29, 2004, against Paraguay in a friendly between U-20 teams. Upon learning about the unusual (and bargain price) sale of the legendary object, Christian assured that his "dream" would be to give it to *La Pulga*: "So that history returns to those who make it," he asserted.

FILM STAR

Lionel Messi was chosen by the Michelob brewery to promote one of its products during halftime in the National Football League's Super Bowl LVII, featuring the Kansas City Chiefs and the San Francisco 49ers at Allegiant Stadium in Las Vegas, Nevada, on February 11, 2024. Leo starred in a 60-second commercial for Michelob Ultra beer, in which he was seen playing soccer on the beach with several people and a dog and interacting with actor Jason Sudeikis and former Miami Dolphins quarterback Dan Marino.

UNCONVENTIONAL PATH

Lionel Messi was the first Argentine player to join the Albiceleste team without ever having played in his country's First Division tournament with a local club. Later, this situation would be repeated by, among others, goalkeeper Emiliano Martínez—who played in Spain and England—and Alejandro Garnacho, a Madrid-born, nationalized Argentine forward for the English club Manchester United.

AN EASY RIDE

The 2024 MLS regular season was a smooth ride for Inter Miami: the Florida team took first place in the Eastern Conference by eight points over the second-placed Columbus Crew. The squad, led by coach Gerardo Martino, won 22 games, drew 8, and lost just 4. Lionel Messi's performance was crucial, as he scored 20 goals despite not competing for two months due to a left ankle injury from the Copa América final. Throughout this first stage of the tournament, *La Pulga* achieved five doubles (against Orlando City, Nashville SC, New England Revolution, Philadelphia Union, and Columbus Crew). He also scored a hat trick against New England, in the last game of the regular phase.

BEST FIFA AWARD

January 15, 2024: Lionel Messi received his third Best FIFA Men's Player award. Leo became the soccer player with the most trophies since the award was created in 2016. Messi, who had already won the 2019 and 2022 editions, beat Portugal's Cristiano Ronaldo and Poland's Robert Lewandowski, who had each won it twice.

COPA AMÉRICA

Between June and July 2024, Lionel Messi led the Argentine national team to win a new title: the Copa América, jointly organized by CONMEBOL and Concacaf in the US. The team, led by Lionel Scaloni, got off to a good start: on June 20, at the Mercedes-Benz Stadium in Atlanta, they defeated Canada 2-0. In that match, Leo did not score any goals, but broke a record that had been held for 70 years by the late Chilean goalkeeper Sergio Livingstone for the most matches played in the continental tournament. *La Pulga* reached 35 matches, one more than the legendary keeper of La Roja. Chile was the second rival of the Argentine team, at the MetLife Stadium in New Jersey. Messi—who suffered an injury to the adductor muscle of his right leg during the match—also failed to score in the 1-0 victory that qualified the Argentine team for the second phase of the tournament. After resting for one match, which Argentina won against Peru by 2-0, Leo returned to the team to face Ecuador in the quarterfinals. In a very tough 1-1 draw (the tricolor team wasted a penalty and a very clear attack when the match was ending), both sides took part in a penalty shootout. Leo missed his, the first of the series: he fooled goalkeeper Alexander Domínguez by lightly touching the ball underneath, causing it to go up. But the ball struck the crossbar and bounced out behind the goal. Fortunately for the Argentine captain, Emiliano *Dibu* Martínez saved two shots—by Ángel Mena and Alan Minda—and four of his teammates—Julián Alvarez, Alexis Mac Allister, Gonzalo Montiel, and Nicolás Otamendi—scored their own to help the Albiceleste squad advance to the semifinals. On that occasion, Argentina repeated its 2-0 against Canada, thanks to another goal from *La Pulga*.

This group never tires of competing, of trying. It is a great achievement to play four finals in a row. Let's enjoy what we are experiencing. We have to take advantage of it because these are the last battles."

(Lionel Messi's happiness when being interviewed on the edge of the field after the Argentine national team beat Canada in the semifinal of the 2024 Copa América in the US.)

BITTERSWEET

The final between Argentina and Colombia, held on July 14 at the Hard Rock Stadium in Miami, had a bittersweet taste for Lionel Messi: the Albiceleste squad won 1-0 in extra time—but without Leo, who had to leave the field at 65 minutes due to a severe sprain. The injury actually occurred at 33 minutes, when *La Pulga* tried to throw a cross from the left, almost on the goal line. With his right ankle injured, Messi received assistance from the Argentine team's kinesiologists, who applied an anesthetic so he could continue on the field. But, at 63 minutes, with the score still 0-0, Leo stepped awkwardly and fell to the ground. *La Pulga* immediately asked for a substitution—a new sprain had aggravated the injury and he could no longer continue playing. Sitting on the bench with ice on the injured joint, the Argentine captain burst into tears. An hour later, at 112 minutes into the game, Lautaro Martínez scored the match's only goal, past goalkeeper Camilo Vargas. The injured ankle did not prevent Leo from returning to the pitch to receive the Copa América and celebrate the new title with his teammates from the Argentine national squad.

LIONEL MESSI AL FACHRI

Lionel Messi played for the Indonesian national team. No, it's not a joke: a boy named Lionel Messi Al Fachri, a player for Akademi Sepakbola Intinusa Olah Prima FC in Jakarta, has been shortlisted for the squad that competed in the qualifying stage of the U-17 Asian Cup in Saudi Arabia 2025. The young lad was born on 6 May 2008, when Leo was already shining at FC Barcelona and had won the U-20 World Cup in the Netherlands in 2005. But unlike the Argentine star, Al Fachri is a defender . . . and he didn't shine for his country's national team: he was left out of the squad that traveled to Kuwait to compete in the qualifying tournament.

RETURN

A sprained right ankle kept Lionel Messi out of competition for two months. During that time, Leo was unable to participate in four MLS matches (he had already missed five others due to the Copa América) and four League Cup matches, from which Inter was eliminated by Columbus Crew. *La Pulga* returned to the Miami team on September 14: that day, Inter defeated Philadelphia Union 3-1 with a double from their number 10 star. Inter not only finished in first place in the Eastern Conference of the American–Canadian league tournament, but they also topped the general table of the regular season, earning the MLS Supporters' Shield.

NUMBERS

Players with the most Copa America appearances:

Player	Country	Games
Lionel Messi	Argentina	39
Sergio Livingstone	Chile	34
Zizinho	Brazil	33
Victor Ugarte	Bolivia	30
Paolo Guerrero	Peru	28

ATLANTA UNITED FC

Inter Miami's strong start in the MLS was halted in the first playoff match. The pink team could not overcome Atlanta United FC, who beat them after three games. In the third, Lionel Messi scored a goal for his side, but the Florida squad still lost 3-2, knocking them out of the competition. Curiously, Gerardo Martino, Inter's coach, had won the MLS in 2018 as coach of the Atlanta team.

MOST VALUABLE PLAYER

December 6, 2024: MLS named Lionel Messi as the winner of the Landon Donovan Award for Most Valuable Player for the 2024 season. The organization noted that Leo's magic was instrumental in helping Inter Miami accumulate 74 points, the highest number obtained by a team during the regular season in the MLS history. The pink club broke the record that New England Revolution had established in 2021, with 73 points.

FINALS

Lionel Messi has played in ten finals for Argentina. The first was in 2005, when the South American team defeated Nigeria 2-1 in the decisive game of the U-20 World Cup in the Netherlands. Two years later, *La Pulga* was part of the team that lost 3-0 to Brazil in the final of the Copa América in Venezuela. In 2008, Leo and the Argentine squad also beat Nigeria, albeit 1-0, to win the gold medal at the Beijing Olympics. The next disappointment came at the Maracanã in Rio de Janeiro, when Argentina lost the final of the 2014 World Cup in Brazil to Germany, 1-0. In the 2015 and 2016 Copa Américas, Messi and Argentina fell to Chile, in both cases on penalty shootouts. The losing streak ended after the 2019 Copa América in Brazil, where the Maracanã provided the Albiceleste team with revenge, as they defeated Brazil 1-0. In June 2022, Argentina won over Italy, 3-0, in the Finalissima, a match between the champions of America and Europe. A few months later, *La Pulga* was crowned world champion in Qatar, after an electrifying 3-3 draw against France and a dramatic penalty shootout. Finally, in 2024, Messi starred in his tenth final, and his sixth victory, against Colombia, in the Copa América in the US.

We are a team and also a family."

(Beautiful sentiment posted by Lionel Messi on his Instagram account after the Argentine national team won the 2024 Copa América in the US.)

CHARITABLE WORKS

Some altruistic gestures by Lionel Messi have been mentioned in this book, but not all of them. Most of Leo's charitable actions have not been made public at the request of the player himself, who prefers to keep a low profile and maintain a modest demeanor. One of those that has come to light describes *La Pulga's* empathy with the people who surround him in his daily activities. In November 2016, the AFA was in the middle of institutional and economic chaos. Without a formal president, the entity was in the hands of a "normalizing commission" that did little to organize and even less to straighten things out. Despite the administrative problems, the team was participating in the Qualifiers for the 2018 World Cup in Russia and had to face Brazil in Belo Horizonte. When the team arrived at the hotel to prepare for the South American classic, a group of employees—responsible for the team's equipment, food, and security—requested a meeting with La Pulga, in his capacity as team captain. "We haven't received our salary for six months," one of the workers announced to Leo. "The situation is complicated. You are the captain of the team, you know us, we ask for your help," the workers' spokesman continued, according to various media reports. Messi then called his father and he immediately made a bank transfer for the amount owed by the AFA to the club's staff.

DID YOU KNOW?

Lionel Messi has his own fragrance. Produced by an Australian company, the Messi Eau de Parfum is "inspired by the man who is more than a soccer icon: this scent captures the essence of Messi's humble but powerful persona."

LIONEL MESSI'S TITLES IN PROFESSIONAL SOCCER

With FC Barcelona:

Champions League (4): 2005/06, 2008/09, 2010/11, and 2014/15.

La Liga (10): 2004/05, 2005/06, 2008/09, 2009/10, 2010/11, 2012/13, 2014/15, 2015/16, 2017/18, and 2018/19.

Copa del Rey (7): 2008/09, 2011/12, 2014/15, 2015/16, 2016/17, 2017/18, and 2020/21.

Club World Cup (3): 2009, 2011, and 2015.

European Super Cup (3): 2009/10, 2011/12, and 2015/16.

Spanish Super Cup (8): 2005/06, 2006/07, 2009/10, 2010/11, 2011/12, 2013/14, 2016/17, and 2018/19.

With PSG:

Ligue 1 (2): 2021/22 and 2022/23.

Champions Trophy (1): 2022/23.

With Inter Miami:

Leagues Cup (1): 2023.

MLS Supporters' Shield (1): 2024.

With the Argentine National Team:

World Cup (1): Qatar 2022.

Copa América (2): Brazil 2021 and US 2024.

U-20 World Cup (1): Netherlands 2005.

Olympic gold medal (1): Beijing 2008.

Finalissima (1): 2022.